KU-392-127

Saturday night... Monday morning

Roger T. Forster

Inter-Varsity Press

Inter-Varsity Press
38 De Montfort Street, Leicester LE1 7GP, England

© Roger T. Forster 1980

All rights reserved. No part of this publication may be reproduced, stored in a retrieval system, or transmitted, in any form or by any means, electronic, mechanical, photocopying, recording or otherwise, without the prior permission of Inter-Varsity Press.

Unless otherwise stated, quotations from the Bible are from the Revised Standard Version (copyrighted 1946, 1952, © 1971, 1973 by the Division of Christian Education of the National Council of the Churches of Christ in the United States of America), and used by permission.

First edition 1980

ISBN 0 85110 412 6

Set in Linotron 10/11 Bembo by Input Typesetting Ltd, London

Printed in Great Britain by
William Collins Sons and Co Ltd Glasgow

Inter-Varsity Press is the publishing division of the Universities and Colleges Christian Fellowship (formerly the Inter-Varsity Fellowship), a student movement linking Christian Unions in universities and colleges throughout the British Isles, and a member movement of the International Fellowship of Evangelical Students. For information about local and national activities in Great Britain, write to UCCF,
38 De Montfort Street, Leicester LE1 7GP.

Contents

	Preface	4
1	Monday morning	5
2	Saturday night breakaway	9
3	Love is . . .	22
4	Who on earth is God?	34
5	To hell with God	45
6	Dead end?	60
7	The beautiful people	82
8	In the end . . . God	99

Preface

Saturday night . . . Monday morning. We can all recognize these as symbols of our human dilemma – the dream and the reality. As we go about our daily grind there is in each of us, perhaps, the yearning for something bigger, wider, freer. We live for the 'weekend', not as reality tells us it is, but as we dream it ought to be. This is what this book is all about.

These chapters were born out of my attempts to communicate the relevant and reasonable Christian message in varied university situations, sharing with thinking men and women who are asking questions about life. It was while I was such a student myself that I made two surprising discoveries: first, that Christianity did not require, as I had supposed, intellectual suicide, but had reasonable and profound answers to give to human problems, and secondly, that Jesus Christ is really alive. I offer these pages in the hope that others might make the same discoveries.

In sharing my faith with others I have become profoundly grateful for the many men and women whose lively minds and intelligent questionings have stimulated and challenged me into deeper Christian truth and living.

My sincere thanks go to my friend and typist, Violet Moon, who has spent many painstaking hours on the manuscript and to my wife, Faith, whose literary flair and meticulous checking have made the book far more presentable and readable than it would ever have been otherwise.

Roger T. Forster

1
Monday morning

Monday morning . . . and your head is as heavy as the skies. You stumble out of bed and draw back the curtains. The rain is spattering down and it's still a bit misty outside. It seemed a good idea to break out of the rut on Saturday night and live it up on Sunday, but now sober reality has descended on you like a ton of bricks.

You take a deep breath as you look into the dim uninviting streets and you screw yourself up to say, 'It's good to be alive!' But deep in the pool of your subconscious something stirs, sending up bubbles which explode into your conscious mind with those persistent questions, '*What is it really all about? What am I here for? Where did the whole business come from – the rain, the streets, the boss, the lectures, my friends – the universe? Where did it all begin?*' And there are really only two answers to that question. Either it didn't come from anywhere, for it has always existed; or else the universe had a beginning.

You creep back into bed to consider these two alternatives (the horizontal position aids the blood supply to the brain, as we all know):

Eternal universe?

Let us suppose the universe has neither beginning nor end. Time stretches infinitely backwards and forwards. Space, which is made up of energy and matter, bowls along this eternity. Energy has always been there in some form or another. The whole system of time and space had no beginning; we have an *eternal universe*.

Now, if I want to know what it is all about and where my part is in it, then of course I have got to try to find that meaning by looking into everything there is. Since there is nothing beyond the eternal universe, I stand here and I look into time and space, and I try to understand what it is all about: Is anything coming back to me? Is there a voice? Is there a god? Is there a world . . . a soul . . . something that speaks back to me? Or is there some totality of which I am a part which registers in my being and says, 'This is it!', something into which I can lose myself . . . or define myself? Can I find a formula or some unifying principle?

Some people think *happiness* is the principle that holds everything together, and only as we live on some 'happy trip' do we really fit into the scheme of everything else; that is the only meaning of existence. But then St Francis was happy as he preached and loved and did everything that seemed to be pure and good; on the other hand, Count Sade was happy in cruelty and gave his name to sadism. So how can happiness be the sole principle that governs and determines every action? One man's happiness may cause another's misery.

Or one may look into time and space, and say, 'I see some *inevitable dialectic* at work, dividing all things into positive and negative, into a thesis and an antithesis; then comes an explosion and a synthesis takes place, until polarization follows again.' Hegel, followed by Marx, claimed this was what was to be found.

Others have looked into the universe and said, 'No, I have found something else: an evolving principle that is making men into gods, and soon *superman* will arrive on the scene, as Nietzsche prophesied, and then the human race will enter into its real majesty as "supermen become gods".' So the suggestions go on.

The sombre opinion of most twentieth-century thinkers, however, as they look into time and space, is that there is absolutely nothing there, nothing at all. Empty, meaningless! All you can do is to make your own choice and live for that for as long as you wish, then abandon it and choose something else; for there is no meaning to man, there is no meaning to existence, there is no voice that cries out and tells me what it is all about and why it all is.

But of course there is another possibility.

. . . or eternal God?

If the universe has not always existed, then it must have had a beginning. This is the only other answer to the question you asked when peering blearily out of the window murmuring, 'Where did it all come from?' This seems to fit in much better with our present scientific knowledge, for energy is coming to a steady state throughout the universe. Our uneven distribution of energy suggests that the universe hasn't been running down for an infinite amount of time, for otherwise it would have reached its maximum entropy by now. It is a perfectly legitimate presupposition to suggest that the universe began at a certain point.

Now, if it began, that is, if both time and space began together,[1] then we have to ask the rider, 'How did it begin? Did *some*-thing – this vast universe – come out of *no*-thing? Is some-thing only constituted of no-thing, or does that defy our very reasoning processes?' We make such distinctions between something and nothing, somebody and nobody; surely something could not have come out of nothing.

So, if there was a beginning, there must have been a Beginner in some form or other. We are not proving God; we are just making a presupposition, that something – call him GOD for the moment (we won't say much more about him than that) – existed eternally. Not an eternal universe this time, but an eternal *God*, who made time and space. This is where the Bible begins: 'In the beginning God' – an eternal God outside of time – 'created the heavens and the earth' – made space, energy and matter. That presupposition is equally if not more reasonable than our first one.

[1] Since Einstein it has been accepted that space and time seem inextricably bound together. See Lincoln Barnet, *The Universe and Dr Einstein*, pp. 70, 19.

But it also brings in another avenue of investigation if I am to discover why I am here and for what I was made. Because I don't only have the universe to investigate, but I also have the one who began it. Is he able to tell me what it is and what I am? If it was begun by something or somebody, then presumably that one can break in to give me his mind, his thought, his purpose, why he brought the whole thing into being in the first place. This 'break in' is what the Christian means by the word 'revelation'.

Let us put it this way. Imagine you are going around one of our new laboratory set-ups, with all the wonderful instruments and paraphernalia of scientific equipment around. You want to know what it is all about, so you ask somebody there, an enthusiastic devotee of science who is not quite over his sixth-form omniscience. He is only too pleased to tell you what it is all about. You say, 'Excuse me, can you tell me *why* this is here, and *why* that is working that way, and *why* this is doing this thing . . . ?' You go round with him, getting the answers to your questions about the various pieces of equipment and the experiments in progress.

Then you find a highly advanced apparatus in one corner – an old battered kettle over a bunsen burner. The kettle is boiling away merrily, and you say to this fellow, 'Excuse me, can you please tell me *why* this kettle is boiling?' 'Oh yes, it is perfectly simple: gas is mixing with air, combustion is taking place, because energy goes into the water in the form of heat, making a vapour of greater volume than the water.' 'Yes,' you say, 'but *why* is the kettle boiling?' And he says, 'This *is* why it is boiling.' And he continues, carried along by his erudition, through all the technological processes of how the coal was taken out of the earth, how it was transformed into gas, how that coal was under the earth because some diluvian forest sank beneath the swamps in some primaeval situation, and how the forest came into being from some protoplasmic globule . . . . 'Yes,' you interrupt, 'but I only wondered why the kettle was boiling.' He says, 'But I am telling you!'

Despairingly you turn to a jaded-looking fellow leaning

on a broom in the corner (the lab. assistant, of course, who runs the place), and you say to him, 'Excuse me, can you please tell me why this kettle is boiling?' 'Why yes, of course, mate, I want a cup of tea ' – an equally good answer, if not better if you are feeling thirsty.

The first answer is a perfectly legitimate one as we look into time and space with its cause-effect reactions, which explain the 'why?' of how. But for the 'why?' of purpose, the meaning of entities, the meaning of that kettle boiling, we have to go to the person who put the kettle on in the first place. And if someone did set the universe in motion in the first place, if there is an eternal God, then it makes sense to ask him what it is all about.

But here, on this bleak Monday morning perhaps, he seems light-years away. You can see the universe but you can't see the Person behind it all. Who is he? Where is he? Why is man so far from him? Why do I feel so alone?

2

Saturday night breakaway

It's a familiar scene in any culture, that old restlessness, 'Saturday night fever', call it what you will. 'I want to break loose, live it up. I want to do my own thing, be answerable to nobody. I want to live my own life, do as I please. I want to be *free!*'

Freedom. The age-old quest of man, whether it is Moses and his liberation march from Egypt in the second millennium BC, or Mao and his 'Long March' in our own century. The frustrated tears of childhood; the aggression of the adolescent; the 'angry young man', anti-establishment, anti-tradition, anti-authority: all these are strivings after freedom, the prize of true manhood. The very word calls forth a response from the depths of our being. Yes, man wants to be free.

Politicians offer freedom in return for votes. Roosevelt stated the Western objective in 1941 in terms of four freedoms: freedom of speech and worship, freedom from want and fear. In the East, the 'People's Liberation Army' swept through China on its 'freedom march' and so on to 'liberate' Tibet and Sinkiang. Some define freedom in the permissive society; others, as in Mao Tse-tung's dictum on political power, 'in the barrel of a gun'.

Modern art, too, pursues freedom. It has largely discarded the old 'classical' forms, so that the artist is free to express himself in whatever way he chooses, even – perhaps particularly – if he does no more than assemble the contents of the garbage can.

But it is philosophy that lies behind art and politics, and modern philosophy offers the ultimate in human freedom – freedom from God. God has been removed from the picture and now men can truly be free without any limitations. Camus remarks, 'We are aliens in a hostile and illogical world.' Man must therefore choose his own way and authenticate himself. But at least, we may feel, he is free.

Freedom come

Jesus well understood this longing of the human heart.

Like all good revolutionary leaders he offered his followers freedom, but first he had something to say about what freedom is and what it is not. He did this in very homely, easily assimilated terms, so that no-one could fail to grasp his point. He told a story. Remember, a crowd was gathering round Jesus as he gave this anecdote. His face, his attitude, the very atmosphere and glow of his personality would come through the words as the people listened. In the background there were his antagonists, because there were and are many who seek to negate what

Christ is teaching. Nevertheless Jesus, never afraid to be controversial, spoke on:

A man had two sons. When the younger told his father, 'I want my share of your estate now, instead of waiting until you die,' his father agreed to divide his wealth between his sons.

A few days later this younger son packed all his belongings and took a trip to a distant land, and there wasted all his money on parties and prostitutes. About the time his money was gone a great famine swept over the land, and he began to starve. He persuaded a local farmer to hire him to feed his pigs. The boy became so hungry that even the pods he was feeding the swine looked good to him. And no one gave him anything.

When he finally came to his senses, he said to himself, 'At home even the hired men have enough and to spare, and here I am, dying of hunger! I will go home to my father and say, "Father, I have sinned against both heaven and you, and am no longer worthy of being called your son. Please take me on as a hired man." '

So he returned home to his father. And while he was still a long distance away, his father saw him coming, and was filled with loving pity and ran and embraced him and kissed him.

His son said to him, 'Father, I have sinned against heaven and you, and am not worthy of being called your son – '

But his father said to the slaves, 'Quick! Bring the finest robe in the house and put it on him. And a jewelled ring for his finger, and shoes! And kill the calf we have in the fattening pen. We must celebrate with a feast. For this son of mine was dead and has returned to life. He was lost and is found.' So the party began.[1]

In this story Jesus came straight to the point of man's basic problem, which is that in his attempts to find freedom he has severed the essential link that a creature has with his creator. The young man virtually says, 'Father, I wish you were dead.' (You don't usually get the inheritance until Father is dead, do you?) He didn't put it quite

[1] Luke 15:11–24, Living Bible.

as bluntly as that but that is what it amounted to. 'I wish you were dead. Can I have my inheritance and then I'll be off. I want to be free from all these petty restrictions that bind me up in your home. I want to break loose, to be myself, to find out what it means to live. Father, give me what is mine so that I can be free.'

In such down-to-earth terms as these, Jesus is highlighting the problem of the whole human race: we want to be rid of a Father God and his restrictions, to break out of all the God-talk lying over our society, all this restrictive background of 'this is right and that is wrong; this is the definition of man; stick within your limits, don't break out into new things'. We want to be free. Like the young man in Jesus' story, we feel we have a right to our own life without the restrictions of a Father, however loving. Consciously or unconsciously, we want God out of the way.

It is no modern phenomenon to wish God dead or indeed to be an atheist; there have been plenty such in the history of the world. One thousand years before Jesus Christ came, King David wrote about those who say 'there is no god'. In the sixth century BC the Chavakas of India were atheists. Buddhism in its classical form is fundamentally atheistic. The Epicureans generally espoused that viewpoint of life. And Epimenides who was a Cretan prophet wrote, '*They built a tomb for you, O high and holy one; . . . but you are not dead, For in you we live and move and have our being, and you remain for ever.*' Epimenides, some centuries before Christ came, was saying of his compatriots that they would build a tomb for God, if only they could get the high and holy One in it!

Then Jesus came, claiming to be God's extension into the world, the Son of God, God communicating with humanity. It was inevitable that he should come to a violent end. If it were not a crucifixion it would be an electric chair, or something of that order. We do not want God interfering too much in his society. It is not really his world of course, it is ours, and we don't want this intervention. So Jesus was violently discarded out of our world.

God is dead

At the end of the nineteenth century, Nietzsche coined the popular phrase, 'God is dead'. Others took up the tune and whether from rationalistic or existential philosophy the cry came: God is dead. At last some theologians, perhaps anxious to catch up with the times, felt in the 1960s that maybe it was time they re-interpreted Christianity in the same terms. God is dead, we were told; this is the good news. God is dead, so we can be free. And as we dance upon his tomb at last we men can become whole men, men become as gods!

The atheist Sartre takes more seriously than the cheerful, *avant-garde* theologians the terrible and solemn meaning of a Godless universe when he says, 'Yes, and this is what it means: it means "total responsibility in total solitariness"'; for he sees more profoundly that we are not what God is. If God is dead, everything is on our shoulders and we are alone. So our art paints it thus and our literature breathes the message, our pop songs take on the minor key so that 'the leaves that were green turn to brown', and our personal relationships, like Cathy, get on the morning train and disappear, for that is all there was to them. We have lost something fundamental. Unfortunately sometimes it requires an atheist who is true to his own presuppositions, whether a Nietzsche or a Sartre, to scream in the ears of mankind that the world is a desperate place, if indeed God is dead.

Perhaps we thought that with our great ability, strength and prowess, at last it was time, as another expressed it, we rolled the God-boulder right off the human scene and pitched it over the precipice into the abyss; but we had forgotten that we are tied inextricably to that boulder and the rope is not limitless but fast running out. Suddenly a yank comes on that rope and we too pitch over the precipice. It is no longer just God who is dead, but man also. There is no destiny for the human race which has pitched its creator over the precipice of oblivion. Man dies with his God.

It is exactly this picture that Jesus, twenty centuries ago, sought to put before us in terms of a family situation. Here we have the young man striding out of the house, saying, 'To hell with Dad; I'm finished with him. I want to live in a country far away from him.' When at the end of the story the boy returns, his father says, 'My son was dead, but he is alive again; he was lost, but is now found.' For it is when we can solve this problem of the deadness of God to us and our experience that we discover that man has come alive again too. It is only when we put God back in his place, at the foundation of all things, that we discover that man can be something after all.

Not that the onus is entirely on us. This God that we try to repress is continually seeking to re-surface in our consciousness, taking us by surprise when we least expect it. In the first century when Jesus came as God's revelation to man, and was crucified accordingly, it was inevitable that somehow or other his grave should burst open and men and women should discover that Jesus was alive again. For the God who showed himself to us in Jesus Christ really is involved with the human race; that's why he became man, wrapped up in our very cells and chemicals, with our sort of psychology, with hands like ours to work with and feet to walk with. He is the God whose heart beat into the human scene, the God who moved into our affairs with compassion and love, talking, working, laughing, crying, dying – yes, the God who entered into our very dying! It is the same resurrection God who keeps disturbing our complacent consciousness and saying, 'Look, I'm still here! How about coming home?'

Man is . . .

Jesus seems to pierce through the cloak of our indifference and penetrate each of our hearts with his story of the lost son. He gets to the root of our problem and shows that individually we do matter. It is not just a sociological answer, though of course Christianity has implications there; it is not just a political answer, though Christianity is bound to make itself felt in that area too; it is not just a philosophical answer. Rather is it a personal answer. The human race is made up of individuals. If individual man counts for nothing, then the whole human race counts for nothing, for 4,000 million times nothing still equals nothing. It is an idealistic fallacy to assign to mankind *en masse* personal attributes such as a will, mind, value and rights, while denying these to the individual. If there is no help for us individually there is no help for the human race.

This is why Jesus made his message a personal one, put in terms of personal relationships. Like the son in the story, we have rejected the origin of our being, cut ourselves loose from the source of our life, and are dying in our attempts to go it alone. If this particular disease in us personally cannot be stemmed, the epidemic which is world-wide will never be solved. The recovery begins with each of us finding the answer in this area with Christ, allowing his healing to take place in our own human experience, until there begins to be the corporate impact of men and women who are discovering a new life and life-style, lived now with the source of all things, God. This health is released into the society of the human race, affecting all; but we contribute to mankind's well-being only when we have got the problem put straight in ourselves.

The boy leaves home. He is going to be himself and find freedom. 'I've cut loose from all this Father business now; yes, I have got my resources. No, I don't know where they came from exactly; I suppose it might have been Father, but I don't think of him too often.' A quick glance round to see if he is cutting a good figure in the eyes of others, but unfortunately he only catches a glimpse of his father's face, with pain written in it. Father is saying nothing; he has probably said enough already and has no more to say. Love cannot coerce; it must let go. Nevertheless it hurts the father, for will he ever come home again? If he does, what will he be like? Will he have hurt himself irretrievably?

In the far country where the son seeks his emancipation, there is free, riotous, relativistic living – permissivism – living with no guidelines, no absolutes, pleasing oneself. He may have had momentary twinges of reason: 'How can you be sure you are being yourself if you don't know what you are meant to be?' After all, I might decide to abandon the usual human process of walking and decide that I want to be a bird. If I don't know what I am then I'm free to be what I choose; I can authenticate myself. So I take off from the edge of a cliff and frantically wave my arms, attempting to fly, only to discover too late that, like it or not, I'm bound by the inevitable consequences of gravity. Ecstatic moments of being released, as I dive over the precipice, evaporate as I hurtle down into the dead-end-ness of the destruction of my own human nature and personal being. This is what the Bible means when it says 'the wages of sin is death'. If we define freedom as 'doing as we please', it destroys us. Define it as 'being what we were meant to be' and we experience freedom and life within the limits of our created design.

The young man in Jesus' story must have had moments when he threw himself on his bed in disgust or dissatisfaction after some new experience which he had hoped would liberate him. He dreams fitfully in the night and at times remembers the face of his father, some distant memory he has repressed.

In the unconscious of every man there lies the image of our Father's face, the face behind the universe, which now and then emerges through our subconscious mind, seeking to surface into our very consciousness if we would only allow it. Nietzsche described a 'sea-sickness, as we go our troubled way without outside help through the world'. Sartre wrote on the subject of man and called his book *Nausea* – the sickness of just being human. But perhaps in such moments we might have a more profound intuition and call it, with Helmut Thielicke, 'homesickness' because it is a symptom of being far from 'home'. We have lost our roots, and there is no foundation to our being any more.

In the nausea of homesickness we are remembering the face of our Father. We don't always know it for what it is of course, but it is that ache that occurs when we are alone on a mountain; or when the sun sets and we want to worship and don't know what to worship; or when we wish that some childhood or adolescent experience would return again – if it did return we know it would not satisfy us as it did then but still there is some ache within. So we ache and we are sick, and we know there is a Face behind the universe trying to get through again – you know the moments. We can dismiss them again with various arguments or, when we wake up in the morning, reach for a couple of aspirins. Nevertheless there have been such times when we have been confronted with our own real sickness.

We have lost the Face that is behind everything, and so we too are becoming faceless. We can try to escape by abandoning ourselves to our unrestrained impulses. But after a while we are unable to control ourselves any more, for our chemicals take over. What we hoped would give us good dividends, such as some new sex experience, some lust after power, perhaps the greed for money, experimentation in drugs, violence, the occult, finally overtakes us and we are controlled by our own cells, our chemicals, rather than by our own choice. We are not really free at all. Sartre perceptively observes that even abandonment to chaos and meaninglessness, all that is left without God, is in itself a bondage.

Nevertheless we still press on; after all, we can't stop. Maybe one day these experiences will throw up the ultimate that we are waiting for – so we wait on. But there is not even a glimmer coming through to assure us that there is something at the end of the road. So then, inevitably there is that terrible business of having to go on play-acting – as the intense student, perhaps, or the budding intellectual, or the woman who knows how to handle things, or the fluffy-headed thing, or the religious type: we all have our parts to play. We don't know who we are; we don't know what we are meant to be; we are like dead men trying to find an identity; beings who are lost in a vast world, not sure what we were ever meant to do or be.

The homecoming

Who am I? I remember a girl screaming this out one evening. She played one thing before her parents and another before her friends, entered into various relationships which had not brought her any real satisfaction. Now she was screaming in a moment of abreaction as she re-lived the experiences of her meaningless life, 'I don't know who I am! I don't know who I am! I am one thing here and one thing there, endlessly playing a part.'

C. S. Lewis, in his book *The Great Divorce*,[2] shows us the end of that drama. He describes a man continually playing a part, building a sort of caricature of himself which he carries around in his pocket on a chain, taking it out every now and again when he wants to impress someone, get into a particular bit of society, control his wife or show off in some scene. The more he takes out this caricature and makes it perform, the bigger it gets, until at last, instead of it being controlled by the chain, it is controlling the diminishing man on the other end of it. Lewis concludes his picture by having the caricature growing so huge while the real man continues to dwindle, that eventually the caricature stoops down, picks up the real man and swallows him; now there is nothing left. We play a part because we don't know what we were meant to be and now it is 'exit' for the real man.

Sadly, we rarely take account of our ultimate meaning or of God until we are lonely and hungry. Out in the fields, the central figure of Jesus' story was given work, but nothing to eat. He was so hungry he would have eaten the pigs' food. After all, if he was just a clump of chemicals, a materialistic beast, he might as well live like an animal. Somehow, though, that answer didn't seem to solve the problem. There is more to man than just animal responses. So his hunger grew. Now Jesus comes to the

[2] C. S. Lewis, *The Great Divorce* (Fontana, 1971).

punch-line, perhaps the most profound point of the whole parable:

'And when he came to himself . . .'[3] – when he discovered who he was – 'he said *"Father* . . . I will go to my *Father".'* When he breathed out that one simple word 'Father', he realized his identity. For it is when men and women dare to open their mouths and say 'Father' that they make the most profound discovery of their being: 'I was meant to be a son.' That is why I am play-acting a thousand parts, because I don't know what I was meant to be; that is why I am trying to wrest meaning from my chemicals by giving in to the basic urges of my being; that is why at times I find a rising up from my sub-conscious of a kind of sickness related to something else behind it all – I was meant to be a son of the Father of the universe. When you start to call God 'Father', you are touching something which is most fundamental and deep. I was meant to bear his character, share his life, have rapport with his wisdom, enter into his mind and heart, taste his love, get into his business.

Father and sons is Christianity. Father and sons is humanity, and that is how we were meant to be. We were meant to have that fulfilment of our own personality as it encounters and involves itself with the Person who lies behind this universe. Jesus tells the story and as we look into his face, he says: 'Any man who sees me has seen the Father – because I am what he is: that is, what the Father does, I do; what he says, I say.' And we begin to understand our potential as sons as we see God's Fatherhood expressed in Jesus Christ his Son.

It is not so much the 'Father' part of the son's confession which we find difficult, however, as the 'I have sinned'. Jesus tells us that the son had to get up and go back to his father and say, 'Father, I have sinned.' Now that *is* difficult. It is one thing to be able to say, 'Father'; but it is another thing to be able to say, 'Father, I have sinned.' It is a confession of need, of wrong; it is an acknowledgment

[3] Literal translation of the Greek.

that I have not been what I should have been, that I have not come up to what I intended for myself, let alone the purpose for which I was made. And the Bible says I was made for God. The fact that I haven't been what I was created to be is entirely my responsibility.

It does not have to be an emotional thing; it is bare factual acknowledgment that I have not been God's son and I have not lived in that character and relationship before him. It is what the Bible in other places calls 'repentance', changing our mind about God and about ourselves, and telling him so. 'I will arise and I will go to my father, and I will say to him, "Father, I have sinned . . .".'

The celebration

It is in that response and confession to God that we find, as Jesus tells in the rest of the story, that the Father comes running down the road to welcome his son – the only place in the whole of the Bible where God is figured as 'running'. Jesus no doubt intended us to see the Father as the older man, falling over the kerb-stones, tripping at the gate if only he can get to that boy of his who is coming back. 'Father, I have sinned . . . I am no longer worthy to be called your son . . .', and before he could get any more words out the Father interrupts him, 'Bring quickly the best robe, and put it on him, and bring the fatted calf.' Dancing, music – that is Christianity! It is when the dance starts; it is when the feast begins; we are in harmony with the heart of our Father and he greets us with a reconciling embrace. We know God is like that for as the Father in the story came running out, so God came out to us in Jesus as he became involved in our world, in our humanity, in our living, in our dying, in our loving. God has come running out to us just where we are, in Jesus. And on the cross God is welcoming us back with a reconciling kiss. He says, I have come to seek and to save. My son was dead and is alive again, he was lost and is found. And so the feast begins.

C. S. Lewis was a lecturer at Oxford University when

one day and for the first time he gave in and 'admitted that God was God'. At that moment he stepped out of atheism into an experience which he later described by the title of his book *Surprised by Joy*.[4] He called it that because, as he said, 'I was the most reluctant convert in the whole of the British Isles.' But when he was reconciled to God he experienced to his surprise the 'feasting, music and dancing' of Christianity; he was surprised by joy. And the man or woman who, having recognized rebellion for what it is, comes back to God and enters into that experience finds that Christianity is as Jesus describes it, even if like the son he might go out next morning into the fields with his father saying, 'I know the music has stopped and the dancing is over and the feast is finished, but, oh Father, it is just so good to be home again! What are we going to do together today? You know, Father, I do love you.'

A non-Christian two decades ago called upon our society saying, 'Where is there somebody who can say, "Hallelujah, it is good to be alive!"?' The exuberance and exhilaration of life which John Osborne sees missing is found by living in the adventure that God will take us into when we come back to him as sons. That link between creature and Creator is restored because we have the courage to come back and say, 'Father, I have sinned; if you can take me back, please do; do something with me, make me free to live.'

The desire for freedom is like a search for some elusive bluebird. An ideal with no reality. But we are truly liberated when we 'come home' to acknowledge our Creator God and live in relationship with him. Then we can answer Osborne – Hallelujah, it *is* good to be alive!

[4] C. S. Lewis, *Surprised by Joy* (Fontana, 1959).

3

Love is . . .

The only value left in life for many people in the twentieth century is love. Yet even as this is asserted, there arises a nasty thought, that perhaps after all this judgment has no place in a thoroughly 'grown-up', 'man-come-of-age' materialistic society. After all, if, as we are assured, there is nothing but matter, chemicals and energy, then our deepest moments of sharing were only the chance relationships of randomly assembled atoms (DNA of course). What really *was* that moment of encounter and enrichment? Love as merely a chemical reaction has no meaning. Victorian 'love without sex' becomes nuclear-age 'sex without love'. If we try to define love as something more than this, we have to introduce ideas of personality or spirit which are not justifiable in a materialistic philosophy.

Jean-Paul Sartre grapples with this problem in one of his stories when the lover lies in bed happily holding his girl's hand – until he imagines the hand amputated and lying on an operating table. 'How can I love an *object* which might make me disgusted?' he asks in revulsion.

It is very often in moments when love awakens and takes hold of our being that we become conscious of another realm, a sphere of awareness and existence where values of love, goodness, beauty, justice, truth and life itself belong. It's a dangerous moment, for if, as is very likely, we are challenged to selflessness, altruism, gentleness, fairness and justice, and if we then choose the reverse for our own immediate self-gratification, the beauty and sweetness, the pure golden enchantment will rapidly fade away. We lose sight of the other person in a self-centred trip where bodies interact but persons never meet, where flesh is exchanged but there is not the enrichment of a little bit of one soul being received and cherished by the other.

Body and soul

In Tolstoy's last great novel, *Resurrection* (in which he describes his conversion to Christ), Nekhludov, his hero, has such an awakening of love. In the presence of his Katusha, everything is just as it should be, everything is beautiful. As beautiful as the Easter day, the day when Nekhludov meets her with the traditional Orthodox greeting, a threefold kiss and 'Christ is risen'. But innocence is soon exchanged for selfishness and she becomes the first of a trail of used and rejected women, or more accurately 'things', in his life. Sex-experienced but love-lost, he finds himself, many years later, sitting on a jury to judge a prostitute accused of poisoning her client. To his horror he sees it is Katusha. To have treated her as but one more object in a materialistic universe, where there had been no real values, had been prudent and sensible, he argued. To continue in the same way now that fortune had made him the judge of what virtually was the result of his behaviour was also the expedient and proper course. Nekhludov nevertheless decides to return in spirit to that Easter day – not as the comparative innocent he was then, but as one disgusted with himself. He first feels disgust by seeing the sin and ugliness in others and judging them. Seeing it now in himself, he enters the spiritual realm of love, truth and life by inviting God into himself to be at one with him and to purify him. So begins his inner resurrection.

Tolstoy is describing what many have found, that human love, while opening the door to the spiritual realm of values, in itself is but a signpost to the existence of the 'Ultimate himself', who also is personal as we are, and whose name is love. The rejection of this Love and his existence spells an excuse for the alternative life-style of selfishness and eliminates the source from which uncreated love can flow. Life lived in this plane of Love may prove, as Nekhludov found, exacting and demanding, but it has a tang to it that makes the self-indulgence kick insipid and a bore.

Nekhludov, or rather Tolstoy, was not the first by any means to come to God asking questions about the quality of the life he had been living. This awareness of deficiency was the source of the question a lawyer once asked Jesus: 'What must I do to inherit eternal life?' Jesus' reply to the lawyer was in effect, 'You already know the answer.' Taken aback perhaps at being put on the spot himself, when he was trying to quiz Jesus, the lawyer quotes the religious law, 'You shall love the Lord your God with all your heart, and with all your soul, and with all your strength, and with all your mind; and your neighbour as yourself.'[1] He knew, as most of us do, that living is something to do with loving and when we love, we truly live.

Living and loving

Eternal life is eternal loving, says Jesus. 'Do this (that is, love) and you'll live.' This for the lawyer is his moment of truth. Is there no way of escape, or must he face up to the issue of eternal and final realities rather than hide behind his moribund shield of profound and intelligent questions? God had said, Love your neighbour as yourself – ah, here was an escape route – 'Who is my neighbour?' (Does that peasant fellow not realize he is dealing with a trained philosopher? I'll make him look small, answering me in these broad generalities. Anyway, he can't expect me to understand that he means any Tom, Dick or Harry who needs a fiver off me!) So '*Who* is my neighbour?' Now, to crown all the indignities piled upon the educated assailant, Jesus answers him with an anecdote:

'A man was going down from Jerusalem to Jericho, and he fell among robbers, who stripped him and beat him, and departed, leaving him half dead. Now by chance a priest was going down that road; and when he saw him he passed by on the other side.

[1] Luke 10:25–28

So likewise a Levite, when he came to the place and saw him, passed by on the other side. But a Samaritan, as he journeyed, came to where he was; and when he saw him, he had compassion, and went to him and bound up his wounds, pouring on oil and wine; then he set him on his own beast and brought him to an inn, and took care of him. And the next day he took out two denarii and gave them to the innkeeper, saying, "Take care of him, and whatever more you spend, I will repay you when I come back." Which of these three, do you think, proved neighbour to the man who fell among the robbers?' He (the lawyer) said, 'The one who showed mercy on him.' And Jesus said to him, 'Go and do likewise.'[2]

'What must I do to inherit eternal life?' the lawyer had asked. 'Eternal life is eternal love,' Jesus had replied. But there are three things which, this story demonstrates, eternal life is *not*.

1. *It is not having the right answer*

The lawyer had the right answer but not the practice or reality of it. Words and ideas can be deceptive. The exchange of beautiful thought and compelling argument can exhaust the energy to live those same things in the daily routine.

This was forcefully illustrated for me one day. I had been chatting to the folk with whom I was working at the time about becoming a Christian and the new life which God offers. One girl picked up what I had been saying of the need to decide personally about the Christian faith, and the difference that it made. She quizzed me about whether this was just a way of describing the general acceptance of a set of beliefs, or whether you could look back and say, '*Then* I became a Christian.' I explained that though there would be many influences and contributing factors, most people would be able to point to a specific time. The reason for her curiosity, as it turned out, was that her father, a university professor of theology, had recently come home and announced that he had been 'converted'. The family

[2] Luke 10:29–37.

were a little confused by this new phenomenon in the learned gentleman and, at that stage, not too pleased about it!

In terms of knowledge and having the 'right answers', this scholar was already at the top of the tree. In terms of personal experience of this central fact of the Christian message, God's offer of eternal life, he was only a beginner.

'What must I do to *inherit* eternal life?' asks the lawyer. Even his question is couched in terms which suggest that he knew intuitively that it must be received as a free gift, as an inheritance. Life, like an inheritance, must by definition be received unearned.

Jesus' answer implies a second thing.

2. *Eternal life is not having the right form of worship*

The priest in the story belonged to the highest category of worshippers in Israel. They led the people in the purest form of God-given services – according to the book! They were not a sect or denomination of Israel either, and certainly counted themselves a cut above the Samaritans and other neighbours whose religion and worship was, at best, a watered-down version of the true, and at worst, a totally unenlightened man-made speculation. In contrast, Israel's religion was from God.

The priest, though advantaged and having a right religion, could not help the injured man and manifested his deficiency – deficient in love and therefore in life. I remember a clergyman's daughter coming to me with tears in her eyes. She was well thought of by all, highly spoken of, she had attended Sunday church worship more times than could be reckoned, she even ran a Christian group in her school. 'I'm not a Christian,' she told me. I tried to assure her that she was but she insisted that she did not have eternal life. So we prayed together to God, the Source of that life, and she received as God promised.

I have seen men arguing about points of procedure in Christian worship in a way that evidenced the absence of this eternal love-life. The history of the Christian church in its sectional squabblings has been abhorrent to any sincere seeker after truth: drowning, burying alive, burning . . . all done in the name of the worshipped Christ who himself said, 'love your enemies', 'turn the other cheek' and 'forgive lest your heavenly Father will not forgive you', 'do not resist evil with evil.'

So the priest must hurry on to Jericho and start the meeting on time; after all, it's bad manners to God to be late for services! But if the priest manifested that he lacked love, what of the Levite, who was the worker and minister in Israel?

3. *Eternal life is not just doing the 'right' thing*

This may sound rather extreme if left unqualified. Obviously 'life' if it is alive must do, or act, and love if it is real love must be active, and presumably it must act rightly: but eternal life is more than just doing the right thing. A dead body connected to the right electrical stimuli could perform certain functions. A computer could produce right results, given the data. However, it would be hard to imagine a computer taking the place of your girl friend as you say to her,

> Shall I compare thee to a summer's day?
> Thou art more lovely, and more temperate.
> Rough winds do shake the darling buds of May . . .
> *etc., etc.*

The reaction of the computer would hardly be the reaction you wished evoked from your girl friend, a reaction (we hope) of love, expressed by the right action; there is more in the action than just the touch of hands, the look of eyes. Love motivates the action and comes through it.

The Levite could not supply that extra. True, he was a worker, a servant in Israel. He came over and looked at the near-dead man and . . . no doubt made a report for the police concerning the geography of the area, the likelihood of robbers causing further incidents, and on the principle of 'prevention is better than cure' he might even make proposals to the Home Office. But now, of course, he must not forget that he had the funds of his newly founded Samaritans' Association with him. He must be responsible with other people's money; the robbers may still be around! Better hurry on. Unfortunately that poor devil there has nearly had it; it's a shame, but we'll do our best to stop it happening again.

When travelling by train a friend of mine began talking with the only other occupant of the carriage, a lady who had been in social work most of her life. She was now retiring and going home to her country cottage which she had refused to enjoy for years, on account of her work in a run-down part of London. She had turned down marriage prospects because she felt her service must come first. But sadly, as they talked, a bitterness became apparent. 'I've given up all my life to *them*', she said, referring to the people of her work area, 'and got nothing out of it.' Not that she went into the service to get something out of it. Not in the first place. Maybe during the years she drove herself with an altruism not expected of her. No doubt she did much to alleviate suffering and deprivation. But as my friend shared with her concerning the source of all good, which is God, as Jesus says in Mark 10:18, tears came to her eyes.

We can't but ask the question, did this woman ever convey to anyone that for which we all ache: love and respect for our real person? The unfortunate patronage that goes with 'service' only heightens the sense of being deficient, non-accountable, unworthy, in the needy recipient. Love, on the other hand, gives the other a value and respect which is man's greatest deprivation: there is nothing a hungry world needs more. Of course it needs bread, but if bread alone is given to the hungry, they will hate the giver for heightening their sense of uselessness and non-value, unless it be given with love. The way of service alone will breed resentment, envy and ultimately hatred; only the way of love has a chance to solve the world's problems.

Dangerous love

After the evident deficiency of the alternatives, the priest and Levite, Jesus now introduces the hero, a Samaritan. Jesus' courage is superb. Look at him, for instance, in the synagogue, healing a man on the sabbath day. He knows the cripple is there as a 'plant' to fault his religious credentials. A withered arm could surely wait until the next day? But his compassion dictates courage and in the face of their hostility, in front of all, he heals him on the spot. Again, in the temple crowds, Jesus tells the Pharisees what somebody should have told them years ago, that they stank! 'Graves full of dead men's bones'! If real love does not gloss over evil, neither does it try to find a soft, patch-up alternative, for in time the emergency repair will come unstuck.

Imagine a Jew today telling a story in Jerusalem about an Arab hero! Conversely, imagine an Arab in Syria saying that where the Arabs had failed, a Jew had proved more praiseworthy! Would either get out alive? Give the story today's connotations. Here is an Arab soldier, at the end of the last clash with Israel, plodding home through hundreds of miles of Sinai desert; he comes across a wounded, hated Israeli calling for help. 'He may hit me if I go near him. He seems genuinely in pain. Here, have the last drop from my water bottle, and if you hang over my back perhaps I can drag you to the nearest first aid post.' A few miles of sweat and he leaves his burden in comfort and safety to face the remaining hundreds of miles of desert before he himself reaches home. Do you see the sort of story Jesus told? It was certainly not sweet, sentimental and mawkish; to recount it was a risk to Jesus' life just as the action of the Samaritan was a risk to his.

During the 1939–45 war the brother of a friend of mine lived in an occupied eastern European country. A Fascist government was in control and many known Communist sympathizers were imprisoned and in severe privation. Obedience to Christ whom he served led this man, though in possession of the bare essentials for life, to make up sacks of warm clothing and food, walk the miles to the nearest concentration camp and, at the opportune moment, throw his sacks over the fencing. At the end of the war the situation was reversed and, with understandable satisfaction, the Communists imprisoned large numbers from the previous regime. My friend's brother repeated his loving actions toward the oppressed and eventually had to flee for his life from the country. He died in the West, his body weakened by the privations endured for the sake of others.

In both sets of circumstances the authorities, and society, found his actions distasteful and out of order: the *status quo* must be maintained, we don't want trouble. But love as taught by Jesus is bold, courageous, inventive, unreasonable, extravagant; it is provocative and non-aligned to the restrictions of class, colour, creed or sectional interests. People, as Paul puts it, are just people made in God's image – not Jews, Gentiles, employers, employees, cultured, uncultured, male or female, but just persons to whom we owe love – not persons conveniently lost in their sectional classifications and thereby depersonalized to others.

It was this dangerous, universal, excessive, non-calculating love that Jesus lived, taught and immortalized in the Samaritan of this story. Dangerous love, for the Jericho road was notorious for violence; universal, for the Samaritan served not a fellow-countryman but a Jew; extravagant, since he paid up and even left a promise for further payment for a man now bereft of everything. 'Take care of him; and whatever more you spend, I will repay you.'

Costly love

Jesus is going to say to the lawyer, *'Go and do likewise.'* Such a challenge is inevitable. 'If you want eternal life, then go and love like that, for that is eternal life, that's what it is all about.' But first Jesus requires a reply from his questioner. 'Which of these three do you think was neighbour to him that fell among thieves?' he asks. At first this question might appear unnecessary, pedantic, even sarcastically cruel, to make the man look silly. Surely it is obvious what the anecdote has taught; need any more be said? But the question is vitally important. Let us look at it more closely.

'*Who then was neighbour* to the wounded victim by the roadside?' Jesus asked. But the lawyer had not asked that question. He had asked 'Who is my neighbour?' but had received in reply the counter-question, '*Whose neighbour are you?*' While I stand calculating, 'Is this wretch in need my neighbour, for whom I might find some love?' the divine question is probing me and bringing its searchlight to bear on my empty heart, Can you love as the true neighbour for which a man such as this looks? He looks for a neighbour to love *him* rather than one to love; he hasn't the resources to love anyone in his wretched condition, but he needs *your* love.

This reversal of the question changes the whole complex. It changes from: Does this man deserve my love? Is he to be treated as my neighbour? to the issue: Can this man find neighbourliness (love) in me, deserved or otherwise?

It is a command to go into such a life-style that Jesus gives in the words, '*Go and do likewise.*' Some years ago a Korean Christian pastor learned that his two sons had died in a school political riot. When order had been restored and the murderers brought to court, the bereaved father pleaded for these young men, offering his home in which the fellows could finish their education while on probation. One young man refused, but the other accepted and the pastor received and loved him in the place of his own boys. Today that murderer is a preacher of Christ's message. 'Where does such love come from?' we might ask, as surely the lawyer asked on the day Jesus said to him, 'Go and do that sort of thing.'

Let us expose ourselves to Jesus' question, '*Which one was neighbour to the man* who fell among the robbers?', and to the inevitable reply, 'The one who showed mercy on him.' Suppose I ask myself '*Whose neighbour am I?*', the sobering conclusion I come to, especially when I hear the command to leave theoretical contemplation and move into pragmatic action – Go and *do* likewise – is that there is not that in me to meet the needs even of the small world of my daily round.

Love is

'*What must I do to inherit eternal life?*' Commending the lawyer for his right reply, Christ gave his authority to the Old Testament statement, which was, in a word, LOVE. But the reply was given in two parts and those parts were in order of precedence: the first was 'love God' and the second was 'love your neighbour'. And the wisdom in this order is that having God brings me into touch with the source, the fountainhead, of all love. God is love and in him I find the resources to love my neighbour, or better still, to be a neighbour to all men in my world. A man becomes a neighbour, that is, a source of love in the world, when he himself takes the God of love into his own being. That is eternal life. Jesus says that it wells up in our life like a spring giving eternal life if we come to him and drink, so that we may really live, and love, in this world. So the ultimate problem is not how can I love my neighbour, or be a real neighbour, but how can I first love God? This is my real difficulty. How can I love a vacuous spirit? How can I love one whom I have never seen? This is the difficulty for most of us, and Jesus Christ claims to be able to meet this problem.

In the story of the good Samaritan we, like the lawyer, have been trying to identify with the hero, but when Jesus commands us to go and do likewise, we give up. We never could be a source of love to our fellows, a real neighbour. When it comes to loving, we identify more with the poor poverty-stricken and dying traveller who needs someone to love him. We need help, and if that help is through loving God, will someone give us a start?

Now no-one has ever seriously claimed that Jesus did not live what he taught. Contemporary first-century critics and those of later centuries generally agree on this.

So if he taught the Samaritan story he must have lived it, and this he certainly did. He said, 'If you have seen me you have seen the Father,' that is, God; and then he proceeded to get alongside dying humanity in his own death, a neighbour to two rejected dying thieves. He lived it as he invaded the God-forsakenness of their death (and ours): 'My God, my God, why have you forsaken me?' he cries on the cross. And all this that he might pay the price to bring us to his Father's resting place, that we might know God. It is when I see the three letter word G O D spelt out, filled out in the terms of Jesus, his living, his dying and his resurrection, that I begin to be able to love God. God is no longer an unlovable abstraction, he is the embodiment, in Jesus, of everything 'Samaritan'; meeting me in the breakdown, rejection and poverty of my dying life, and paying the price of recovery and new life.

None of us can love God, nor even our neighbours, in the way we know we ought. Failure, inability, these are the hallmarks of our life. That is why, as the lawyer saw, eternal life is something we must 'inherit'. In his supreme love God has reached out to us in Jesus and offered not only to pay for the consequences of our failure (the rejection owed to all who have rebelled and ignored God) but, as we respond, to put back together the broken pieces of our shattered human life. He offers forgiveness of our past life and the opportunity of a new life, a God-given capacity for love: eternal life beginning now and lasting beyond the tiny compass of human life as we know it. Such is the 'inheritance' God has provided for us when we acknowledge him as our gracious Father. This is why God's 'grace' – his love for undeserving man – is popularly called 'amazing'!

Learning to love

God's offer of himself to us in Jesus is knowable and lovable. Even so, some of us may say, 'But still I don't know how to start loving God. How does it get off the ground? I don't feel very much, even if I ought to, when

I think of Jesus Christ.' Here perhaps the real issue is the *commitment* that love requires. There was a moment when I stood next to a girl dressed in white and was asked if I would take her to be my wife. I said I would. She was then asked if she would love, honour and obey me, and she said 'I will'. She knew a little about me then; I knew a little about her too, and of course I loved her to some degree at that time. But today, years later, I love her a thousand times more. The commitment to each other, 'I will', resulted in a life together, symbolized by joining hands and walking out of the church together. So, my life of love with God begins with a committal, 'I will'. God has already made his committal in Christ's death, which says, '*I will* have all men to be saved', and he awaits our response.

We know a little of Christ: his life, like the Samaritan's, shows us God who is the source of all love. In loving us he gives us the offer and even the ability to love him, a love that grows with time and knowledge, and leads to loving our neighbour, through this well-spring of unlimited resources found in him. Like the Samaritan, Jesus has done for me everything to make me rich in living, and loving. Such eternal life becomes my experience when I simply say 'I will' to God in his offer of love in Jesus.

4

Who on earth is God?

Where is this God we keep talking about? We can't see him. Where would we look for him? We might just as well look over here as over there, since they say he is everywhere. Even that sounds suspicious – perhaps he is nowhere! Who on earth *is* God anyway?

A friend of mine was preaching in a certain place, and half-way through the sermon a girl jumped up and shouted, 'If there is a God, then show us your God!' He was not too disturbed by this interruption, but afterwards asked who the young lady was. He was informed that she came to the meeting fairly regularly, but being a humanist, rejecting any idea of a God, she shouted out this same thing every week. My friend thought it an interesting situation and asked if she were likely to do a repeat performance when he revisited the place. Being assured that she was, he replied, 'All right, I will be ready next time.' Some weeks later he returned and, true to form, the young lady jumped up, shouting, 'If there is a God, then show us your God!' and sat down again. 'Right, stop everything!' he said, and at his signal a friend entered, dressed up like Father Christmas. When the laughter had died down (and the offended 'pharisees' had got up and walked out) he said, 'If you must ask a stupid question you should expect a stupid answer!' Now that may have been a little unkind, a little unfair. But perhaps I should add that the girl in question did come to discover that God was knowable in Jesus Christ.

Do we really expect anyone, at the drop of a hat, suddenly to materialize God to our vision and say, 'There you are!'? Or do we expect a little door to open somewhere in space and reveal the person who is at the controls of everything? It's reported that Gagarin, having returned from space, was asked, 'Did you see God up there?' He replied that as a matter of fact he hadn't. A little girl on hearing this remarked, 'Well, of course it does say "Happy are the pure in heart for they shall see God".' I don't think she was reflecting too seriously on Gagarin's character! Rather, she was expressing her intuition, which accords with Christ's teaching, that seeing the Spirit behind the universe depends on conditions spiritual and moral rather than the factors of space and time such as the opening of a door to disclose divinity, or even finding it at the end of an infinite mathematical series. Such demonstrations would barely be convincing amongst the multiplicity of sensational shows and technological trickery of our century. Do we really expect some demonstration of God on that sort of level? If we do, I think we are asking a less than intelligent question.

Nonetheless, to be sympathetic to the lady's enquiry, maybe it came from those depths that lie within the heart of all of us, questions born from fears or hopes that, if there is an infinite, if there is a Person, vast and spiritual, behind this universe, could he communicate with us men and women, and if he did, would that communication be intelligible? Is there any way in which there can be rapport between the infinite and finite?

Such a question as 'Show me your god' is a real one. This is especially so if the questioner oscillates between fears and hopes of there ever being a satisfactory answer to his enquiry as to the ultimates, the meaning of life. Perhaps if there is a God he cannot ever be touched and can never be known; and those moments of ache and longing in our hearts, those moments of shame when we feel we want forgiveness, those times when we look around saying, 'Is there some meaning or some purpose?', perhaps they are all just mere mockings of our own hearts and we can seek but never find.

If God had indeed created us with a desire to know him and yet never intended to satisfy that desire, it would be as bad as creating us with a hunger for food yet not providing us with the means to eat. Imagine a futuristic scientist, having discovered how to create life, deciding to create something living – perhaps a flea. Not just an ordinary flea, however: this one has a special awareness, a big question-mark programmed into his little flea heart, so that he hops around saying, 'Is there anything beyond? Is there a meaning to my life? What am I doing here? Can I really love? Is there any value in my existence?' Now imagine the scientist watching the flea with detached interest, then remarking to a colleague, 'You know, he'll never find the answer to his questions because I made him without eyes or ears, so that even if we stand over him and shout, he'll never understand.'

Is God like that? Then we can never know him and never communicate with him. He is the infinite and we are finite. We are at an impasse. Perhaps we had better remain in our agnostic position, for who on earth is this God? Anyway, who would want to meet him? The inhuman scientist deserves to be locked up!

Touching the infinite

Some years ago Arthur Koestler contributed with other disillusioned Communists to the publication *The God that Failed*, meaning, for him, that Communism had failed. He had earlier thrown in his lot with the Marxist dream. He was an Hungarian, an intellectual who wanted also to be an activist. He found himself involved in revolutionary enterprises and eventually was gaoled in Seville during the Spanish Civil War, accused of being a Communist spy. While in prison, anticipating that at any moment he might be taken out and executed, Koestler had a 'spiritual' experience, he tells us in his autobiography.

As he sat there, trying to take his mind off the possibility of his own execution, he went back to his school days and tried to remember mathematical proofs, and these he started to scrape out on the wall of his cell. One was to prove that there is no highest prime number (in other words, that there is an infinite number of prime numbers). As he scraped away on the wall, trying to find the equation, suddenly – and he describes it as a spiritual experience – there came that sort of delight that comes when light dawns and we know that we have seen something that we have never seen before, and joy fills us. There is a momentary moving out of time, and we feel that we are touching something that is final and absolute. He describes it like this although he is not a Christian, and indeed at that time was an atheist. He says it was in those moments that he suddenly realized he had written an equation that proved that there was an infinite number of prime numbers, and that meant that after all, despite what very often he had been told, indeed asserted glibly and cheaply – namely, that you could not make meaningful statements about infinite things – it was possible, because he himself had just done so.[1] Our finite condition, the smallness of our brains and grasp of intellect, can still make reasonable, meaningful statements about infinite things.

Of course it is exactly at this point that the Christian message says, God has indeed made such statements possible, and we can say, We know God. Not that, in a sense, we can grasp the infinite – we can't – but it must be possible that we have some meaningful rapport with him and take in some understanding about him.

If there is a God who can be known at all on earth, he is one who somehow or other can come through from the infinite into the space-time situation in which we live, and somehow or other communicate at our level. The 'coming through' of God we could compare with the music of a magnificent orchestra being reduced to a piano piece: although the piano plays exactly the same melody as the whole orchestra, and nothing of that melody is lost, yet the depth, the profundity and the diversity which exists within that melody can be brought out only by the orchestration of a hundred and one different instruments. In one sense something is lost, but nevertheless the whole tune is there.

Christians claim something of this order has happened between the infinite and the finite, and, as we have seen, it is a reasonable claim. Jesus Christ, as the piano setting of the music of the infinite God, can say, 'My Father is greater than I' but can add, 'He who has seen me has seen the Father.'[2] So St Paul asserts concerning Jesus: 'in him the whole fulness of deity dwells bodily'.[3]

Let us use another analogy. Picture the infinite-dimensional God as a three-dimensional sphere, and human beings as flat men in a two-dimensional plane. The lower scene of existence, our world, would be like a flat sheet of paper, the three-dimensional sphere, which is God, moving through it. A moment comes when the sphere touches

[1] A. Koestler, *The Invisible Writing*, p. 428. [2] John 14:28; 14:9. [3] Colossians 2:9.

down and is seen as a point in the paper; as the sphere moves through the paper, circles begin to be seen in the paper at every phase of the journey through that plane area. We, living in that paper, don't see the whole of the sphere in one moment; but at each section through our universe a circle is seen, and an infinity of those circles makes up the whole three-dimensional object which is making contact with the two-dimensional world. So, as God breaks in to make himself known, something of his infinitude is seen in the circles which we can see in our human realm. In the thirty-three years of the person of Jesus Christ it is claimed that the Godhead was seen, in time and space, in meaningful terms – as the sphere was broken down into circles. God's word, or communication of himself, has been made flesh and dwelt amongst us.[4]

Coming through

The claims of Jesus to deity, then, are not unreasonable claims, for after all, if God is going to communicate with us, how otherwise could he adequately have done it, but by becoming a man? God could speak to us through the very structure of the universe, and there is a certain amount of information one could glean from space and time. Presumably the very logic and pattern of so much in nature – though it does not appear to say too much – could say something to us concerning ourselves and our creator. Or maybe God could speak to us through the very beauty that exists, but there is a certain amount of ugliness too, and it leaves us perplexed. Or perhaps he could speak to us through our consciences, because he has given us this ability, when we say: Well, that is wrong, and that is right – especially when we view others' actions or political stances. Unfortunately conscience, so often, can be determined by environment. My mother used to clip me round the head every time I took too much butter when I was young; so when I take my own butter these days and put it on my

[4] John 1:1, 14

bread, I still feel that inward clip round the head. That is my super-ego; that is my conditioned conscience.

How could God really communicate? He could become a great mountain or tree or something; but that would only say he is rather big or that he blows in the breeze. Maybe he could become an animal and snuggle up against my knee? Well, that would only tell me he is rather snuggly and warm. Of course, there is only one door open when we think about it: if God is going to communicate to man so that we can know something of why he made this universe, who God is, what he is like and what we are here for, it can only be done if he comes on to the particular wave-length which is ours, and he becomes a *man*. And the reasonableness of it all is evident in that we didn't even have to open a Bible to discover it; we could have just sat down and thought, and it might have come through. There is only one real way in which ultimately God can communicate with man: it is by having a heart, hands, brain – a body that enters into the very scenes we are in and therefore speaks our human language.

If we accept that God would communicate with man in this way, how would he go about it? Would he just suddenly appear on the scene without preparation? It isn't likely. Such a profoundly important revelation as God's ultimate communication with man would require careful preparation. Maybe he would start with one man, say, a man like Abraham, with whom God could communicate by means of dreams and visions, and even more deeply, inwardly, through his spirit and conscience. From this man, and his family, God could build up a whole race who would keep the revelation entrusted to Abraham, and to whom God could continue to reveal more and more of his ultimate purpose. When God did then make himself fully known in the person of Jesus, there would be a nation able to comprehend what it was all about and who Jesus was. Israel was that nation. Thus God prepared the environment of his revelation for centuries beforehand.

Now when at last he came into this world, would he enter by the normal process of birth? To do otherwise would make him something other than man. He would need to have a normal birth and a normal nine-month foetal experience if he were going to be a full man. Yet inevitably there would be something unusual about the way he came in. Do you remember our 'sphere and plane' image? Take the point where the sphere breaks into our two-dimensional world (as we called it in our illustration), that point of contact is where the seed is planted in the womb of a woman, a virgin conception. It is minutely small and entering at the only point available if this man is to be a full human, going through all the processes: gestation, birth, growing up, maturing, forming relationships. It is said of Jesus that he grew in wisdom and knowledge.

And we would not be surprised, would we, if this 'God as man' did a miracle or two, for, after all, it would not be a very full revelation of God if he did not show his creative power. So we would expect him to do one or two miracles. We would expect him to do a bit of teaching of ethics. His teaching would not be really 'way-out' stuff, because it is only cranks who introduce new ethics; it would be the sort of teaching which, by and large, we men realize is the right sort of way we should live. (We don't necessarily do it, but we know we should.) He would confirm our natural ethics and perhaps deepen them, although his theological teaching might be a little unusual!

Interference

However, if he really were God, we would have to throw him out again; we could not let him go through the whole span of life without rejecting him. After all, we don't like God around too much, do we, frankly? I don't. You don't. He wants to interfere; he wants to get involved in our lives. He might argue that, as he started the whole process, he has got a say in the way we are going. We don't like that sort of interference; it brings in antiquated ideas like – 'you have got to obey the source of everything if you are going to fit in to the programme.' Obedience is an ugly word to us. So, inevitably, we shall have to throw him out, and we do it rather violently. We would expect him to be executed. Even Socrates prophesied that if a perfect man were to come to this world then we would execute him. Of course Socrates might have been a little biased – after all, they did make him drink hemlock!

But if this man, who is the revelation of God, died, we would not expect him to remain dead, would we? If he is God – eternal life is not dismissed so easily. Don't be surprised if, somehow or other, he brings up this fantastic story of breaking open death itself and coming back again. I mean, if those elements were not in the story it would not be a reasonably valid story at all; it would not fit in with the reasonableness of the whole case. If there is a God and if he has communicated to this world, the very story of Jesus Christ is such a reasonable claim for the event that we would be staggered if some of these elements, and particularly that one of resurrection, were not found in it somewhere.

He could not, of course, come back and do it again and again, because there is absolutely no rational basic evidence that man does come back again and again and again. We are talking of incarnation, not re-incarnation, for the evidence of such for mankind does not exist. He lived one man's life, died once, rose again once – and that was it.

Of course we can overlook him and ignore him and pretend he was not there, and never would be there, but the unfortunate thing is that the harder we try to run away, the faster God seems to interrupt us with his resurrection-Jesus; he keeps cropping up when we thought we had got rid of him for good and all, asking that we make some decision about him. And the very reasonableness of his claims, even the offer of his forgiveness is a prerogative which belongs only to God. Jesus said to various people: I don't condemn you, go and sin no more . . . I forgive you . . . she loved me so much because she is forgiven . . . and so on.

Had we been close associates of that person Jesus – his friend Peter, say – we might also have responded when we looked at him, 'our God and our Saviour'.[5] Had we been a Thomas, who followed him and saw him die, in the moment of his appearance in resurrection we too might have fallen down and cried, 'My Lord and my God!'[6] Or we might have pronounced with the apostle Paul as he looked back on the historical Jesus of Nazareth, that he was 'our great God and Saviour Jesus Christ'.[7] We would have acknowledged Jesus as God in time and space.

Loud and clear

Now that is exactly what Jesus is claiming; it is exactly what he proposed as he stood amongst men and women. 'He who has seen me', says Jesus, 'has seen the Father.'[8] We might retort, 'But we are looking at a man'; yes, but you see the Face behind the universe – God in man's terms. 'I am the way' to God, 'I am the truth' in human truthful propositions about God, 'I am the life' of God expressed in human life, that you might be able to understand that life.[9] If it were angelic life, or bestial life, or any other of the thousands of forms of life that God could create or has created, we scarcely would have understood it; but reduced to the terms of our grasp, Jesus is claiming to be the I AM. He claims equality with the unseen God; and he says, I always do what he is doing;[10] I always say what he is saying;[11] I am always being what he is being.[12] He says, If you love me you will love my Father. If you believe in me you will believe in God. He equates obedience to himself with obedience to God and he says, If you honour me you honour my Father. He stood before men saying, Come, follow me, and put me first, before mother, father, brother, sister – and the dearest and deepest relationship to which we commit ourselves as men and women. He makes this claim, which would be insufferable if he were not indeed the One who made all relationships, saying, 'You must love me more than . . . and follow me.' He taught things on his own authority – 'I say unto you', and

[5] 2 Peter 1:1. [6] John 20:28. [7] Titus 2:13. [8] John 14:9.
[9] John 14:6. [10] John 5:18, 19. [11] John 8:28. [12] John 10:30.

he would go to the Old Testament to correct the interpretations they had of what they believed was God's truth without paying any lip service of respect to the previous expositions. He said, 'But I say to you . . .', and with humility and yet authority he took the place of the Lawgiver himself – the One whom the Jews who were listening believed had communicated his will to Moses, and whom they were meant to revere. He accepted worship.

Whatever area it was that Jesus touched, his claims were comprehensive and total: He claimed to be the I AM in person, in human terms. C. S. Lewis writes: 'The discrepancy between the depth, sincerity, and may I say the shrewdness of His moral teaching, unless He is indeed God, have never been got over . . . . We cannot patronisingly look at the teaching of Jesus Christ, and say, Yes, He was a good man and quite a good teacher, for He did not leave us with that alternative. He is either on the level of a man who thinks he is a poached egg, a raving lunatic, or he is an arch-demon deliberately deceiving mankind, OR, as He claims to be, He is God.'[13] Mad, bad, . . . or God? Lunatic, liar, . . . or Lord? The person of Jesus Christ demands a verdict.

The Jesus life

Of course, this creates a problem for us today. If men of the first century in Galilee and Judea could see Jesus, God communicating with men, getting on our wave-length, speaking our language – the *Word* which was God and was with God becoming flesh and dwelling amongst us – if they could see him and hear him and understand him in his birth, in his life, in his teaching, in his death and in his resurrection, and thus receive the *Word* of God coming through to them, – what about us today?

Perhaps that is where the most startling part of the story takes place, and that, perhaps, we would not have guessed. For God offers to take the Spirit of that *Man* (which he was) and put that Spirit, that light source, that life power,

[13]C. S. Lewis, *Mere Christianity* (Fontana, 1970), p. 52.

that motivating drive, into each one of our lives; and he calls that his own life, eternal life, because it belongs to the eternal God, or the *Jesus* life, the life we saw in Jesus. And that life, living in his people, to a greater or lesser extent, goes on saying something like the same things, and tries to live out the same sort of life and bring the same sort of communication. And that is why Christians – you may have heard – are called the *body* of Christ, for the very life that is in Jesus is put into his people, and we start to show it out all over again. Christ, we say, lives *in* the believer. And that is what a Christian is.

5

To hell with God

Death – anyone's death – raises in most thinking people the question 'Why?'. The younger the person, the more attractive, vital, gifted, promising they were, the more insistently that question hammers into our brain, '*Why?* What is the point of it? What waste! What a senseless negation of everything good! Why did it have to be?'

When Jesus died in the prime of life, at the height (seemingly) of his powers and popularity, having brought such hope to so many, the same questions slammed into the consciousness of his followers and almost shattered them. Yet Jesus himself had taught them that his death was not only inevitable, it was essential. He was born to die.[1] His disciples came to understand, and then to preach with such power, that the crucifixion of Jesus Christ was the fundamental root of his message.

The cross has become a world-wide symbol for Christianity. Christ called his followers to take up their crosses

[1] Matthew 16:21.

and follow him. Paul said that he gloried in the cross of Christ.[2] Remembering that the cross was the Roman Empire's foulest and cruellest gibbet – only fit for slaves – isn't it a sick mind that can take delight in such a torturous death? The stench and blood, agony and sweat, of such an execution can surely only excite the morbid interest of a perverted, dehumanized individual.

Truly there is something very offensive in Christ's message of crucifixion. A modern writer speaks of it as the 'gospel of gore' and suggests that we emphasize the beauty of Christ's life and teaching while passing over this repugnant article of faith. There is something in us that responds to such a suggestion. After all, true religion should emphasize the beautiful and living, and try to eradicate the dark and seamy side of truth. Thus many have tried to revamp the message of Jesus and remove that which is offensive to sensitive, sophisticated and squeamish twentieth-century minds.

The seamy side of life

The problem of such a renovated, updated message is that there seems to be very little of Christianity left. After all, a third of the gospel material (Matthew, Mark, Luke and John) is centred on the event of the crucifixion or the preparation for it. Jesus said he had come to give his life as a ransom for many.[3] The whole gospel material flows toward this point. This is not because the first century in which it was written was less mature or sophisticated than ours, and consequently found the death of Jesus a less offensive subject. On the contrary, a graffito of the early church period has been found depicting someone worshipping the head of an ass on a cross, with the inscription 'Alexamenos worships his god' – a cruel jibe by his fellows at a Christian's obnoxious faith. It seems it was no easier for an early believer than it is for one today to cross this initial grotesque and psychologically offensive barrier when trying to communicate his faith to others.

[2] Galatians 6:14. [3] Mark 10:45.

Had you gone to the intelligentsia of the day who boasted their Greek culture, you would not have found an easy acceptance there either. To go to those who delighted in the refined excellence of man's body, mind and aesthetic aspirations – who said that in the perfection of mind and body we have the answer to the world's needs – to present to them Christ crucified as an object of worship was asking for outright repudiation. The Greek culture could never be expected to accept that the answer to the predicament of men and women was a crucified criminal, Jesus Christ. They would have stumbled (as Paul said[4]), been offended at the offence, the stumbling-block of the cross. For Calvary spells death to the pride of man that presumes that we in our majesty and development and maturity can solve the predicament of the human race. It declares that we need a blood sacrifice in order to find an answer to the problems of the world, and that was abhorrent to the cultured Greek.

Even if you went to the most religious people of the day, the Jews, with their genius for religion, and declared to them that God's answer to man's need was the Lamb of God that bore away the sin of the world on the cross of Calvary, you would inevitably have faced objections and distaste, for it was in the Hebrew sacred writings that a man who was hung on a tree was evidently cursed of God.[5] How could you expect a Jewish religionist to be moved by a message that said: God himself has spoken to the world through the blood of Jesus, through the death of one who was hung on a tree?

In the first century the message of the cross invited the hostility of the governing power, the intelligentsia, and the religious leaders. Yet Christians were so fired by the magnetism of the cross of Christ that they could not stop talking about it. They told of Christ dying at Calvary crying, 'My God, my God, why have you forsaken me?'[6] In that cry of dereliction and desolation, they said, God is answering the cry of the world and meeting the dead

[4] 1 Corinthians 1:18–23. [5] Galatians 3:13 quoting Deuteronomy 21:23.
[6] Matthew 27:46.

situation of humanity. They were fired with the love which the blood of the cross seemed to spill out into their experience. There was something about it that made them, every time they began to talk about Jesus, very soon add, '. . . and he was crucified, but God has raised him up'. It was the fundamental issue, and still is today, of the true Christian message – *Christ died.*

Despite its apparent distastefulness and lack of sophistication, despite the suggested unhealthiness of people being taken up all the time with death and blood – despite all that – the event of Jesus' dying has been a magnetic point for men and women through century after century, especially to those who have desired to understand the meaning of life and death. Even Rousseau, no friend of Christianity, compared the death of Jesus with that of Socrates, for Socrates died as a wise man: taking the cup of hemlock from his executioner who was weeping, he blessed him, and turning to his friends he sought to comfort them. His was the death of a sage. But the death of Jesus as he hung on the cross midst hatred and shame and spitting, as he cried out in desolation saying, 'Father, forgive them; for they know not what they do', 'that', says Rousseau, 'is *the death of a god*',[7] something superhuman, something that takes you by surprise. Muggeridge calls it the most significant death of history. The great nineteenth-century preacher, Charles Spurgeon, died saying 'My theology becomes very simple – Jesus died for me.' Even the Christian who understands very little about his faith knows the fundamental truth grasped by his own spirit that makes meaning and sense out of everything that he is experiencing in his Christian walk. Yes, Jesus died for me. There is something about the death of Jesus Christ which is compelling and commanding. It makes us look, even if we don't want to. 'I, when I am lifted up from the earth,' says Christ, referring to his execution, 'will draw all men to myself.'[8] We have to take it into account. What does it mean?

[7] Vernon C. Grounds, *The Reason for Our Hope*, pp. 34, 35.
[8] John 12:32, 33.

Getting involved

One meaning is clear enough. Jesus died for sinners, we say. Well, he really did! He loved the harlots, the quislings, the tax-collectors and the ordinary people who were not counted for much and certainly were not religious. It was because Jesus did love those sorts of people that eventually he had to die. He died because he was concerned about the prostitutes, whom all decent people resented because of their threat to stable families and their resultant luxurious living. He died because he loved selfish traitors who made themselves rich by taxing the ordinary people on behalf of the foreign occupation. Any liberationist, moralist, religionist or socially conscious reformer could see Jesus was only fit to die. He died because he would love rejected people, who knew that they needed help, love, reintegration, and above all, God. He died for those who themselves knew, and everyone else knew, were sinners. They listened to what he had to say and wanted to share the health and the love that he was pouring out to men from his own presence; they wanted to know God, or copy somehow or other the way that he seemed to walk as a man; they wanted to live on this earth in the right way – even though they hadn't before. Those are the people for whom Jesus died. In fact, in a sense he died for all of us with any need – and that is everyone, if only we understand ourselves aright.

Sometimes the New Testament writers struggled with the Old Testament pictures of sacrifice. Sometimes they used first-century legal terms, like 'to justify' or to make right: Christ died to make us right with God. Sometimes they used the word 'propitiation' which has to do with exhausting wrath, so that God's reaction to man's sin can be in some way or other worked out and exhausted in order that we might come into the peace of his heart. Just as light always reacts to darkness to destroy it, God always reacts to sin to destroy that. But somehow God has found a way in the death of Jesus whereby his reaction fell there and he is able to welcome enemies as friends. It is evident that the New Testament writers are being stretched, with the help of God's Spirit, to explain and to get to the depths of this terrific event.

Yet there is still a mystery in the cross. That is not surprising because what was happening on the cross was not something which arose out of man's ingenuity or speculation, nor an invention of the human brain. On the contrary, it was something which was born out of the mind and heart of God. It was God who devised the plan to get involved with man, to get involved with his death, so that somehow or other he could open up a gate in our very death and declare life through himself.

It is impossible finally to plumb the total meaning of the mystery of Christ crucified, but we may still benefit from it. The nourishment of a good meal can be experienced and profited from without a total grasp of the nutritious value in terms of calories, carbohydrates, proteins and vitamins.

None the less, two things come through loud and clear. One is that the crucifixion of Jesus Christ, although making available something for all men, must be participated in *personally*. Paul puts it like this: 'The Son of God, who loved me and gave himself for *me*';[9] or John can write: 'God so loved the world that he gave his only Son, that *whoever* believes . . . ', and again, ' . . . So must the Son of man be lifted up (to die), that *whoever* believes in him . . .'[10] 'Whoever' – this is the individual personal response that is necessary to this event of the cross. For if Christ prays, 'Father, forgive . . . '[11] there is the need that I personally should come and drink the sweetness of that forgiveness and make it mine. Then I can begin to say: The Son of God loved *me* and gave himself for *me*. As an individual I start to be involved in the effects of Christ's crucifixion. Calvary must be personally appropriated, so that I can say with Paul, it was 'for me'.

Secondly, what comes through loud and clear is that Christ's crucifixion has something fundamentally to do

[9] Galatians 2:20. [10] John 3:14–16. [11] Luke 23:24.

with *sin*. Sin de-mans our 'mannishness', for it is a break-away from the definition that God has given man. We step outside the boundary of our definition when we resent, when we are bitter, unloving, brutal, base or lustful, and our true human nature is destroyed. That is sin: disobedience to the God-appointed definition of what it means to be a human being. This definition is perfectly measured out in the humanity of Jesus; coming short of that beauty in our lives is sin, and it is in the realm of sin that we must understand Jesus' death. Paul says 'the wages of sin is death'.[12] Christ died because of sin – not his, but ours.

Moral blackmail

There are those who object to the Christian message of Christ dying for the world by saying that it is a kind of moral blackmail. Christ died – well, it forces you to make some sort of response to him, out of sympathy, out of sheer decency. There is a sense in which that is true. When I became a Christian, it was primarily seeing Christ dying that moved me to some responsive action. I felt, 'Well, I must do something about it.' So it is sometimes charged that this is moral blackmail, as though God did something (if it is true that he did) which forces us to respond out of sheer humanity. If he went to such lengths to show me his love, we might say, then I had better respond.

Now that would be blackmail if it were not that God was also doing something necessary *for us* when Jesus died. Let us put it like this: Suppose you were going for a walk with your girl friend, along the side of a fast-flowing river. You are no swimmer. You say to your girl friend, 'My dear, I love you so much, how can I declare to you my love? I love you absolutely passionately; I love you so much I would die for you. Now just watch!' And you dive into the stream and sail down the torrent. The last she sees of you are the bubbles that arise in the distance! You could say, 'Well, there you are, that just shows how

[12]Romans 6:23.

much I love you' (but you wouldn't say it because you would not be there to say it!). However, I don't think she would be particularly impressed. She would probably say, 'Well, it's a good thing he did not become my husband and the father of my children, because he would have been thoroughly irresponsible!' I don't think she would be too impressed by the quality of your love.

In the death of Christ, God is not just showing how much he loves us – at least, not that alone, although that is true. Let us rather put it like this: suppose the girl falls into the river and her lover then pitches himself into the torrent; he can't swim, but he just manages to push her to the bank, and with his last push falls back himself. Once again the bubbles rise to give evidence that this lover died for the loved one. Now the girl, for the rest of her life, would say, 'Yes, that fellow really did love me.' Whatever happened to her afterwards, no matter whom she gives herself to, she would say, 'That man really loved me. He gave his life to save mine.' What Jesus is doing at Calvary is not just making a great demonstration; he is dying man's death; he is getting into the predicament that we are in, in order to extricate us. That is why we declare that in the death of Christ we see the depth and the height and the breadth, indeed, the whole measurement of the love of God. He did something about our predicament that is going to save us.

Gospel of gore?

There are those who say that they don't like all this blood talk, all the 'gospel of gore' stuff. After all, it is a little horrific – why major on the suffering side? Why not just talk about the other?

But let us ask ourselves, Do we really think that God has anything to say to this sort of world, with all its violence, its bloodshed, its bitterness, privations and oppression, that does not have to be spelt out ultimately in all the bloodiness of the cross? In a bloody world we need a violent message; and the violence of Calvary is God speaking to men and women who need to know that in this world there is a God who has met that violence and taken the blow on his own heart. If God had not spoken to us in the stark terms of blood, then we twentieth-century products with all our ability to destroy and to hate would never listen. The human blood that has wastefully flowed in rivers down the centuries would have nothing to answer it from an almighty God, unless he speaks in that *milieu*. Man might invent some vague idealistic song, but that would be no realistic message for dying and violent men.

It is in the blood of the cross that God is speaking to our hellish world. Don't forget that it *is* hellish to millions of people who do not sit as we do in the ease of Western culture (although that also is fast eroding and dying). For the majority of mankind life has been a suffering and sad tale, and God has spoken to the world in the cross of Jesus Christ in a way that begins to make sense in such a scene.

Some of you will have read Ernest Gordon's book *Miracle on the River Kwai*[13] or will have seen the film *Bridge over the River Kwai*. They both relate the same time and event in the history of the last war, when prisoners of war were used in Burma to build in one year a railway which should have taken six years. They were beaten to work on this crash job; consequently they were dying like flies. Their conditions were hellish. There was no time to think about anybody but self if you were going to stay alive in that concentration camp. Day after day men saw their friends turn against them, betraying them to the guards, stealing the few things they had left, just for the sheer . . . 'Well, I had better look after Jack because nobody else will!' It was a terrible situation, but one or two unusual things began to happen on that camp. A few Christian men lived in a way that made people talk. There was the Scots fellow, for instance, who regularly took his food down to his mate who was dying in the sick quarters (men in the sick quarters were not fed because they were not able to work). One day Jock died, debilitated with malnutrition. They had

[13]E. Gordon, *Miracle on the River Kwai* (Fontana, 1965).

told Jock he was a fool to keep giving his food to a dying man. But his friend lived; Jock did not. It made people talk.

There was a time when a platoon was thought to have lost a tool. They were all marched out and the guard shouted and screamed that every one of them would die unless that tool was given back. Nobody moved. He shouted again that every one would die; he cocked his rifle and looked down the sights. One man took two paces forward, implying 'I took the tool'. The club of the rifle came down on his head and he was beaten mercilessly to death. The platoon was marched back into the camp to the tool-shed. The missing tool was hanging in its place; it had never been missing. One man had given his life for his friends – something like Jesus did, on a mini-scale. Men asked, 'Who was this fellow?' He was a Christian.

In this situation, which was as near hell as it could get, the men went to an officer and asked, 'Do you have a Bible?' The officer said he had. They replied, 'We want to know if Christianity has anything to say to us in this scene.' The officer said, 'Supposing we read it and find out that it hasn't?' The men answered, 'Then at least we will know.' So they read and studied the Bible every night. A spiritual revival took place amongst the men. Many of them came out of that camp as Christians, including the author of the book *Miracle on the River Kwai*. In Christ's cross God has something pretty straight to say to a violent world. If he had not, there would be no message for us at all.

Immorality?

The writer of that book about the River Kwai miracle had formerly thought, like many, that Christians spoke in terms of an angry father sending a loving son to die, who somehow or other appeased the anger of the father, and thereby brought men to heaven. This seemed to him immoral. But this, too, is a misleading caricature of the meaning of the cross of Christ. The Bible declares that God himself was in Christ, reconciling the world to himself. The event of the crucifixion was not something to induce an unwilling God to be favourable towards men by the action of a third party. It was God's action. What God was doing, he was doing in and through Jesus Christ. That death was something which God himself accomplished.

What then is God saying to us through the death of Christ?

1. *What sin does to man*

When we look at the crucifixion we see a mangled body, twisted and in pain. Now, let's be real – you must have seen blood at some time; perhaps you have seen a car accident; you must know the horror of a twisted body and the agony of the human frame. God points to the cross, that most horrific of all executions and says: That is what man is. That is what sin does to man, spelt out in the symbol of our flesh and blood, but expressing the very torture and agony of our personal souls. That is the dehumanizing that sin brings to the human frame, shattering human personality and breaking the spirit as it cried in desolation, My God, my God, why have you forsaken me? In the moments of his execution Christ cried that desolate cry, depicting the very hell that exists in the human soul, and which cannot be extricated by man's therapy – the hell of shame and guilt, of lust and pride, the hell that burns within us and will go on burning even when our bodies have been stripped from our person. Hell begins in the human frame; and Jesus experienced it on the cross. God points to Calvary and says: That is what sin does to man.

In one of Christ's stories, he tells of a man who died and went to hell,[14] He speaks of the thirst which the man longs to be slaked. If we thirst now, we shall thirst for ever, unless God can somehow get into that hell and salvage us out of it. Perhaps there have been moments already in your life when you have troubled to stop and ask yourself questions about love, when you have wanted to act altruistically and haven't been able to. Hell begins in the

[14]Luke 16:19–31.

human soul, and God has gone to hell to get us out of it. That was what he was doing on the cross.

Sartre (who was of course an atheist) tells us his definition of hell:[15] Three people find themselves sitting in a cell. They can't get out, there is a bright light and they are condemned to eternal sleeplessness. So they begin to chat with one another. It all starts quite nicely at first, but as they go on chatting they begin hurting one another. Suddenly, one of them realizes: 'This is a kind of economy in devil-power.' She says, 'We are in hell but each of us will act as torturer of the others.' The others scream and shout, demonstrating that she is correct, while trying to tell her that she is not. Here is Sartre's definition of hell – that though we are confined close together, our personalities are miles apart and never make contact. The terrible, tragic loneliness of the twentieth century is but the overspill of hell. We were meant to be sons of God, knowing his life, sharing his wisdom, entering into his business, knowing him in the family of his love. Hell is the destruction of all that. 'My God, my God, why have you forsaken me?'

2. *What sin does to God*

If the crucifixion shows what sin does to man, it also shows us what sin does to God. For it is God who, in Jesus Christ, is entering into this human predicament. It is God who is taking this blow upon his being. Sin is doing something to God.

I remember some years ago seeing my son being hit by a truck on a road in Eastern Europe. I was unable to do a thing as the vehicle applied its brakes and my boy hesitated slightly, till the wing hit his head, throwing him into the air. I would have given everything to have stood over him or in his place. My father heart was stretched in the agony of those few seconds into what seemed an eternity as the inevitable impact took place. The pain of the blow reverberated in my own psychology – virtually as a physical impact. Thank God, my son lived. Perhaps the blow

[15] Jean-Paul Sartre, *No Exit.*

I experienced helped me to understand in a small way the bruising God sustains in seeing the result of man's sin. It hurts, and it hurt God.

When I begin to see that my living in God's world *my* way, rather than God's way, hurts him, that is often the moment when I begin to say at last: I must do something about it. I must stop and begin to go God's way. It is the broken heart of God that is displayed as Jesus dies – for sin hurts the God of love who made us to be his children.

3. *What God has done about that sin for man*

If the crucifixion shows us what sin does to man and what sin does to God, it also shows us what God has done about that sin for man. In the Old Testament days, when people came to offer a sacrifice, there was audience participation. The worshipper would lay hands on the sacrifice and confess his sins over the animal, and then the animal would be slain. The sacrificer would go back home and continue in fellowship with God. Something happened when Jesus died, which is *for* us and which we cannot do ourselves. In ancient times a man might lay his hands on the sacrificial animal and confess that what was to be done to the sacrificial animal ought to be done to him. Something like this is taking place with the death of our Lord Jesus.

Think of a line of trucks on a railway track receiving an impact. One hits the first, and that one the next, and so on, till the impact bounces all the way down the line. So, in the closed circuit of this universe, sin with its repercussions bangs down from time forward and time backward to the very cross where God has come into time and space. Christ stands as a truck with the brake on, or as the buffers, to take the impact and to exhaust the effects of our sin.

If you saw the film *The Exorcist* (and I don't recommend it for those who didn't!) you will know what a horrific portrayal it is of the supernatural scene today. It is also an expression (though imperfect from a Christian perspective) of the only solution to the problem of evil. The psychiatrist takes the demonic force of the child upon himself, pitches himself through the window and dies, as a *substitute*, to save the child. For 2,000 years the Christian gospel has been declaring that, at Calvary, Jesus Christ is doing that to the power of evil and thereby removing the force of sin from men's lives so that we can become whole again.

Or let me put it another way. A man and a woman love one another and set up in marriage, having a home and children. Later the fellow goes off with another woman, perhaps two or three, but anyway, leaving his first behind. She feels, of course, as though she has been cheated. She feels the pain of it and has to work doubly hard to be both father and mother. Because she loves the man, the desertion hurts her, for she sees what he is doing to himself, as well as the mess he is making of other people's lives. One day there is a bang at the door, and there is her husband standing outside. He stands on one foot and then the other, not looking her in the eyes, more a mouse than a man. He says, 'I'm sorry, will you have me back?' Now, what is she going to do? Will she reply nonchalantly, 'Oh yes, come in. There are your fish and chips, your favourite programme is on the telly, put your feet up!' Is that what she does? If you think so, I don't think you have ever been in love. It wouldn't be as cheap as that, not if you have really given yourself, as well as your body, and see people as people, not things. Rather, there would be a hesitation, a tension inside her.

Suddenly it snaps. Metaphorically she steps forward and stands in his shoes. She feels his condemnation, his self-judgment and fear – 'Will she have me back?' She feels all the consequences of his actions on herself. She puts out her arms – 'Of course I will' – there is a reconciling kiss; a new relationship has been formed. He need never have to fear now that she might reject him once she has discovered everything he has done and been, because she herself has experienced it all in its consequence, and knows what she has forgiven. Now if you forgive someone something and it doesn't hurt, don't imagine you had anything to forgive. It has to hurt, otherwise there is nothing to forgive. When it hurts, that hurt is the evidence that you are beginning to appreciate what it has done to the other person. To some degree there is a rapport. Of course, in our human relationships, it may not be perfect, but to some degree there must be an empathy with that situation.

Once forgiven, never forsaken

What God is doing as Christ dies, amongst other things, is knowing what he is forgiving, that he might say, 'Of course I forgive you; come home.' He died that we might be forgiven, that we might know that we are forgiven, and that we might know that he will never annul our forgiveness and reject us. A new relationship is formed, that of being a Christian. It is based upon the work that God himself has done to be able to offer us forgiveness, having taken the hurt of sin on himself. I know I am a forgiven man because Jesus died for me and I have accepted it. I know that God won't throw me out again because he knows what he has forgiven in Roger Forster. For he bore the consequences of all my sins, in fact, of all men's sins, when Jesus hung on the cross. Christ's death is the basis upon which we can know that we are accepted back into a relationship with God the Father, as sons and daughters in his family. We can begin to live our life on this earth with all the exuberance of the love of his presence, in the delight of his heart over his children's ways.

The cross of Jesus Christ still stands supreme in the final crisis of the soul – the crisis between God and man, the crisis between man and death, the crisis concerning sin, guilt and shame. The cross of Christ still stands supreme – in the crisis of evil, of spiritism and occultism, the powers that wreck the lives of men and women. We know that we have sinned, and the cross has got something to do with that. We personally need to come and say 'Thank you' to Christ for meeting us just where we are. There was nowhere else where he could meet us but in death, for we bear the marks of the death sentence which is written across our human race. A human being knows that inside he is dead, dead to God, dead to love, dead to other people. Jesus meets us just there. He says, 'I died for you.' Come and accept the forgiveness that he offers and the relationship with God which is what makes a man a Christian.

6

Dead end?

You may have one of those modern up-dated Bibles. Some of us who are more used to the older version feel sorry that the modern versions are oftentimes not quite so beautiful, and have lost some of those beautiful nuances. For instance, the passage where the apostle Paul is going to Rome as a prisoner, under guard, and he reaches a place just outside Rome, on the Appian Way; it is called 'Three Taverns'. There, say the Authorized Version, the Christian brothers came out to meet him, and they 'took courage . . .'.[1] It is rather a shame when these poetic touches are lost in the newer versions!

As the apostle Paul proceeded along the Appian Way into Rome for his great trial before the Emperor, he would have passed the tombs of the great and mighty, which still stand there today, tombstones on which are carved the names of the rich, the political and militaristic leaders. Carved on the tombs are little epitaphs which the incumbents have left to society; generally they are sarcastic. One of them, not too far down the road from the 'Three Taverns' perhaps, says: 'A cocktail for you and a cocktail for me. . . And that is life.' That is as much as he could be persuaded to pass on to posterity. You go on a little further, and there is another epitaph, a little more sophisticated; it says: 'Life is constituted of lust, But lust is not good for the constitution' – very profound and helpful, I

[1] 'Courage' is the name of a well-known beer in England.

am sure, for succeeding generations! Another is more sombre; it simply says: 'The sun will rise and set, But it is eternal darkness for . . .' (the man whose remains lie there). Now that is about as much as the great and mighty can say about this world and its life.

Interestingly enough, however, just a few years after Paul passed that way, many men and women who had discovered the reality of the message which Paul proclaimed throughout the world began to be buried in the catacombs, while hiding from persecution. Not all of the graves, of course, have been opened. But those that have, have something to say worth hearing. Some give words similar to Paul's that we can read today in the New Testament writings, such as, 'Absent from the body, present with the Lord.' Another one says: 'To live for Christ – that is good; but to die, that's gain.' Another one says; 'To be with Christ is far better.' All these are verses that are recorded in the New Testament as summarizing what Paul and other Christians were proclaiming throughout the Roman Empire and beyond. For everywhere they went, they did not proclaim some new ethic, some novel system of theology. The exhilaration, the exuberance of their proclamation was '*Jesus is alive*', and soon many other men and women found themselves motivated by the same theme.

Yes, *Jesus is alive*, and somehow or other, men and women who found that it was hard to face life, let alone death, discovered that they could face even death with this theme resounding in their hearts: *Jesus is alive*. Within twenty years of the execution of Jesus Christ (and probably even earlier)[2] people were being buried with this affirmation written on their tombs.[3] Certainly within thirty years of the crucifixion of that peasant leader from Galilee, Jesus of Nazareth – an artisan, a carpenter – men and women were being buried with the hope that somehow or other

[2] AD 50 is the latest date possible.

[3] In 1945 Professor Sukenik, who is well known for his research into the Dead Sea Scrolls, made another outstanding discovery, just outside Jerusalem. There were a number of tombs containing ossuaries, and two of them had written upon them what seem to be these words: *Jesus* – let him arise; *Jesus* – he will help.

their death was not a dead end. They were buried believing that their death was not the culmination of a meaningless existence of loving, laughing, crying and denying, that they had experienced during their seventy years or even less.

Jesus' resurrection had pumped hope into the dead end of man, had pulsated meaning into the emptiness of our human existence. Taking the very dust of the grave he ordered it into a meaningful life saying: Death has been conquered; the victory has come; God has spoken to man's greatest need; the last enemy of man has been defeated.

These first Christians said that Jesus had not just risen from death in some spiritual way, but had actually risen bodily from the grave; walked through a wall, true, but still appeared bodily to his disciples, convincing them he was there. He ate fish off a plate, presumably left the bones on the side, and walked out again. 'What was that?' they might ask, 'Was it a spirit or an apparition?' But when they picked up the bones from the side of the plate, they would say, 'That was for real!' These were the sorts of things that happened. It was not a mystical kind of recycle like the crops that come year by year as the grain dies and comes in a new harvest. It was a resurrection showing that death had been beaten, and it put into the hearts and lives of men and women a concrete reason for their love, for their joy, for their self-denial, humility, peace, self-control: these were seen to be values which belong to a world which cannot be defeated, for it rose again in the person of Jesus Christ and continues for ever.

Now we might conclude that these first-century people were less sophisticated, more gullible than we are today. But frankly I think they would have found it harder to believe in a resurrection than we do. Science has accustomed us to the amazing. You imagine saying to a first-century character, for instance, that if you watch a little box in somebody's front room you can see a man walking around on the moon. He would have said, 'You are a lunatic; we don't believe that sort of stuff; you are not going to con us; we are good down-to-earth peasants; we know what life is all about.' If you had told them that somebody had risen from the grave, they would find it hard to believe. Don't forget that they would have seen lots of people die, would probably have a more first-hand experience of dead bodies than most of us, who veil its reality from ourselves by sophisticated civilized practices. They knew quite as well as we do, if not better, that people just don't rise again from death. And yet, somehow or other they were convinced. Something that they claimed really had happened as an event in history, right down in the midst of our human scene; something which could eat fish and leave the bones on the side of the plate, had changed their whole attitude to life and to death.

Dead or alive?

The whole Christian message stands or falls upon this event in history. If Christ did not leave the grave, if Jesus never rose again, then our idealistic Christian hopes, our attempts at love and selflessness, are really empty and useless. But if Christ did rise from the grave, says the apostle Paul, then our faith is not in vain. Our faith is empty unless Christ rose from the grave, but if Christ is risen then our faith has content. It is not a dream, a speculation, a wish, even a vision: it is *reality* based in time and space, written in the dust of the earth, spelt out in the blood of the cross and an empty grave, and then, and only then, driven experientially and subjectively into men's hearts. There is something real in history authenticating our experience. And so it is inevitable that from the first century to our present day, men and women have sought to destroy the Christian faith by attacking the resurrection of Jesus Christ, realizing that this is a fundamental plank upon which everything else stands or falls.

In the eighteenth century a couple of men decided, when they went up to Oxford, that they would share the attack between them. Lord Lyttleton would write a book to prove that the apostle Paul was never actually converted to Jesus Christ (a bold attempt, if nothing else!); the other man, Gilbert West, decided that he would attack the resurrection, the fundamental plank of Christianity. So each set about his task, not meeting for some years. When at last they met, and asked how each was getting on with his respective work, Lyttleton said, in effect, that he was sorry but he was just not going to get the book out. In fact, as he had studied the material to try and weigh up the case, he himself had been converted to Christ. He was sorry to disappoint his friend! Gilbert West replied that, as a matter of fact, he had written his book but it would be coming out as a book in *defence of the resurrection of Jesus*. You can find the book today in the British Museum, and on the fly-leaf there is a quotation from the Book of Ecclesiasticus (in the Apocrypha), and it says, 'Don't judge a matter until you have examined it' – which is fairly useful advice, I think, when we seek to dismiss certain claims without ever looking at them.

The famous American writer, Lew Wallace, was a general in the American army in the nineteenth century. He was a friend of the more famous Ingersoll, an atheist. Ingersoll said to Wallace one day, 'Now that you have travelled all round the world, Lew, why don't you write a book, one of those books that can really attack Christianity, in a popular style? We have had enough of this hoax of Christianity, beating death by resurrection, and all that; it is time that people had this delusion stripped away from them. Why don't you write in a way that gets the business over to the ordinary man and woman?' Lew Wallace agreed that he would try his hand at it. He started to write his book, calling it *Ben Hur*. One thing he did not take into account was that he had a praying wife – and they can be dangerous! His wife prayed for Lew Wallace until one night he had an encounter with the resurrected Christ. You will know that he wrote his book the other way around, as a popular apologetic of the Christian faith.

More recently in the twentieth century a journalist and lawyer, Frank Morison, took it upon himself to try to hit Christianity in its solar plexus, in order to see the whole thing fall. He tells us in the preface of his book *Who Moved the Stone?*[4] that he set out writing the book to attack Christianity and destroy it by disproving the resurrection of Jesus Christ. In order to be fair to the facts he had to read the material that was available on the subject, in particular the four gospels. As he weighed up the evidence placed before him in those writings he came to the conclusion that the case was a *bona fide* one, and he wrote his book supporting the fact of Christ's resurrection. Jesus Christ said he was going to conquer death. He convinced those who thought he could not do it that he had, and he has gone on convincing people for 2,000 years since, that he has done what most of us would say is really the impossible. We are not likely to be taken in easily with that sort of stuff – unless it is real.

Death – the real thing

Before we spend a little time trying to assess the evidence for this great event in history, let us consider the implications of death, because death is a problem. Don't let us try and hide from it. You know how it used to be: the Victorians would not discuss sex, the beginnings of life, but they were quite happy to talk about death. We, today, are absolutely obsessed with talking about the beginnings of life, but we dare not look death in the face. If we do, we have to cover it up in the most unrealistic way possible, to try to pretend it is not there. We hide behind sophisticated rituals and the expertise of professionals, to remove the evidence from our view. Alternatively, we condition ourselves with such a surfeit of television simulations of death that the real thing, if it should come near us, seems equally unreal. However, if even for a moment we break through this defence and let death's reality touch our lives, we instinctively know that if God has got nothing to say about death, in Jesus Christ, then our faith in him is redundant. Unless a world-view can not only speak about death but also do something about it, it is futile from the outset. Only a faith built on such an answer is going to be

[4] F. Morison, *Who Moved the Stone?* (Faber, 1944).

adequately satisfying for this great problem. For death is a huge problem.

1. *The moral problem*

First, there is a *moral problem* with death. If life can come to such an abrupt and (some would claim) total end, then it throws into question the moral values man assumes. Is there any value in love, in self-denial, in sacrifice, if all that remains of these things, of our human choices, is a handful of dust in the end? Camus tells us, 'That which exalts life to its highest is also that which degrades it to absurdity for it is all meaningless.' If death is the end, then our moral values are worth virtually nothing. Some have faced that presupposition and lived accordingly. But remember that the Christian God claims to meet this dilemma.

Imagine you could talk to a foetus in the womb of its mother, as it is developing little hands, eyes and feet. You might ask, 'Aren't you looking forward to the day when you come forth?' 'Oh no,' he could reply, 'it is much too nice in here.' 'But what about those little eyes that are developing in you?' 'Eyes? I can't see any eyes, in fact I can't see anything. Besides, it is dark; I don't need them.' 'What about those little hands?' 'I don't have to hold anything here.' 'What about those little feet?' 'I don't want to run around, thanks very much!' 'But there is a larger life coming,' you protest. 'There is something bigger and more meaningful for you.'

Similarly, there is a realm where values have meaning and existence, and it is virtually embryonic suicide, it is spiritual abortion, to ignore the reality that God has something larger after this scene for those moral values which we develop in life, growing moral hands, feet and eyes. We are like a foetus that never comes to birth, unless we discover that there is an answer to death, and there is a larger life. Christians claim that there is something which God has planned and prepared for those who, in Christ, go through from this scene into something bigger.

2. *The philosophical problem*

Then there is a *philosophical problem*. Since death is the one certain feature of life, we have to accommodate it in our world-view and it is a problem. In his book, *Dr Zhivago*, Pasternak grapples with the ugliness and problem of death. Zhivago as a little boy looks out of the window and remembers his mother. He sees her grave, tries to imagine his mother alive, and thinks, 'What does it all mean?' Pasternak says that centuries upon centuries of the best of human thought have grappled with the meaning of death, if perhaps we might come up ultimately with the solution, and be able to conquer it. Thus he puts it over in his novel. It is a philosophical problem.

Sartre tells us that all we can do about death is to face it fully in our experience, and come out the other side into a 'horrible calm', as though the very nemesis of it has overtaken our system and life is to be lived in the horrible calm of its ultimate doom. H. G. Wells says, 'If there is no larger life after death, then this life is a huge ugly joke. Man is like an ass braying across the scenes of history.' Is there no answer philosophically?

Sartre and Wells certainly sound a different note from some men who have gone to their deaths with a conviction, even an exhilaration, which somehow or other seems to suggest that they have discovered something more. For instance, there was a man in the Reformation period who was sentenced to death by burning. As his sentence was read out in the courts, he broke forth singing one of the Old Testament songs, Psalm 122: 'I was glad when they said to me, "Let us go into the house of the Lord!" ' Well now, a fellow like that is quite beyond it; you can't do much with him; he starts to sing when you tell him that he is going to die! Either he is terribly deluded, mentally deranged, or he has got hold of something.

Osment tells us in her little book that, as a convinced Communist, she was quite happy with the system until she was confronted by death, her mother's death. Then she began to ask questions which her Communist world-view did not answer. It had nothing to say about this most certain of all life's experiences. She was encouraged therefore to seek further, and discovered Jesus Christ. Death is a philosophical problem, and we need a world-view that covers all experiences.

3. *The psychological problem*

Death is a *psychological problem*, for everybody fears death. I have met and counselled many folk who have suffered from depression and fear following the death of someone close to them. I remember one such young woman whom I met while doing some pastoral visiting in a village. She had not slept well nor been able to go out or care for her child properly for months following the death of her mother. She simply could not shake off the fearful depression that hung over her. I talked with her and read to her the story of Jesus Christ walking on the Sea of Galilee and coming to his disciples in their fear, saying 'It is I. Do not be afraid.' (They had thought he was a ghost or something supernatural from beyond the grave.) When they received him into their boat, they came immediately to the place they had been trying to reach. Then I told this young woman, 'The Lord Jesus does not want you to fear. In fact, the most commanded thing in the Bible is "Fear not". Let's ask God to meet you in this problem.' So we prayed.

When I saw this young woman the next day, she was completely transformed. Her eyes were peaceful and bright. She had found that the living Lord Jesus is able to deal with the psychological problem of death. Now she wanted to know how she could find a lasting, eternal relationship with God.

Professor Jung, one of the fathers of modern psychology, said there was no man over the age of thirty-five who was not living with either a conscious or unconscious fear of death. Of course, like much psychological theory, you can't really test it. For if you said to Jung, 'I don't have a fear of death', he could say, 'But you have – it is suppressed, that's why you don't notice it.' Yet his years of seeking to help man in his deepest psychological problems suggest that this great man in psychiatry should be listened to. We all live with a fear of death, particularly if we have passed the mid-point of our seventy years!

4. *The religious problem*
There is what we might call a *religious problem* in death. For the great world leaders of religion, in all their sincerity and for all the truths that they may have lighted on, still had nothing to say to us about death, in any demonstrable form. Buddha, Mohammed, Confucius, Karl Marx . . . all have their tombs at which you can go and pay your respects. Jesus Christ hasn't! There is no shrine for him. He has no tomb. In fact, we are not even quite sure where it was they put him when they crucified him, for nobody cared too much afterwards. Why go to find a tomb when you can find him alive? You don't go to look amongst the dead for the living.

There is a religious problem, a religious problem that exists and is not answered, either, by some eerie voice from a mediumistic trance. Will any vague voice from some distant shadow-realm convince us that there is a life after the grave? We want something solid, in flesh, with the smell of the early morning on it, the dew and the dust of the earth; and that is how the body of Jesus was when he broke out of the grave on that morning. He came and ate with his disciples. There was earthly reality about it.

Now these are various areas of the problem. If God has nothing to say through the Christian message about the universal experience of death, nothing, I mean, which has a real integral base to it, then really we have no message for a dying world. Death may have its value in reminding us that we are not independent creatures. Drinking a drop of cyanide, or holding on to the end of a high-voltage cable, will soon convince us of that truth! We are not creatures independent of our Creator and death will remind us that there is this problem in our life which needs to be dealt with, to which death is but the final conclusion. For if I deny my dependent humanity, I write my own suicide certificate. Death may even be a mercy, for there must be many people who, when confronted with it, think again.

The answer to the problem of death lies in the physical resurrection of Jesus Christ, giving hope to man that as Jesus was raised from the dead so also God will raise those who trust in him. The resurrection of Jesus is central to the Christian faith, so what evidence do we have of its authenticity?

Resurrection?

The first question that must be answered is: If Jesus did not rise from death, then what happened to his corpse? There seems no doubt that the body of Jesus was missing from his tomb three days after his death. This was an accepted fact at the time, as evidenced by two things:

1. *No 'empty tomb' was preached*
When the first disciples began to preach the message of Jesus after his ascension, they did not once refer to his empty tomb. They said, 'Jesus is alive!' 'Jesus is at the centre of the universe', 'he is taking over all things', but they did not try to argue that his tomb was empty, because it was already a widely known fact. All their hearers *knew* that something had happened to the body of Jesus; the apostles needed only to proclaim, 'God has raised him from the dead!'

2. *No shrine*
If it were *not* for the resurrection message it might surprise us that there is no shrine for Christianity, made from the tomb of Jesus, at which his followers could express their devotion and respect. Despite the fact that thousands were healed or helped by him, or heard his teaching and acclaimed him, yet none seemed to desire a memorial by which to honour him. 'Why seek for the living among the dead?' His followers didn't.

If we accept the fact that Jesus' body was missing from his tomb, we have to ask what happened to it? Perhaps the most popular theory is that the body was stolen. There were several groups who might have had a motive for stealing the body, so we will examine them one by one.

3. *Stolen body theory*

a. The first objection that was made to the claims of the Christians in the first century was that his *disciples* had stolen Jesus' body from the tomb. You can find this in Matthew's Gospel:[5] the guards were paid off to report this story. It is recorded again in the Jewish Talmud: Jesus Christ's body was removed from the tomb by the disciples. Is this a reasonable explanation?

Is it reasonable, first, that a bunch of men who fled when Christ was apprehended and who didn't even stay for his trial were going to go to the only tomb in the whole of Jerusalem that was guarded by a whole picket of soldiers trained in war (and this bunch of men, remember, was made up of quislings who collected taxes, and fishermen who were not trained to use swords and spears)?

Is it reasonable that they were going to try to overwhelm the guards and take the body of Jesus for some unknown reason? And what would they do with it? How were they to get rid of that body of Jesus? (If you have ever tried to get rid of a body you will know it is extremely difficult!) They would have had to get rid of the body and then go around the place saying 'Jesus is alive'.

Is it psychologically possible that those shattered men could find it in themselves at last to stand up before a vast crowd, when they could not stand before one or two soldiers, and begin to proclaim (and ultimately, all of them, even perhaps the apostle John after his long life, gave their lives for this evidence) that Christ was really alive? Ethically speaking, is it possible, without having a psychological breakdown? You must stand up and proclaim to men and women throughout the world, 'This is the message we have: love your neighbour, turn the other cheek, don't tell lies', all on the basis that the story of Christ rising from the grave is the biggest lie yet, and you know it.

Is it feasible that the Christian message could have

[5] Matthew 28:11–15.

spread so rapidly with these disadvantages? Moreover, not one of those men squealed that they knew of any other story! Yet the authorities would have paid them off well (and every man has his price). They would have loved to have got evidence that the body really had been stolen; and yet not one of those disciples (and it ran into hundreds who saw Jesus alive, maybe thousands) ever split on the event, *because they were convinced they had seen the Lord alive*. The tomb really was empty, but not because the disciples had stolen the body.

b. If it were not the disciples who robbed the tomb, could it not have been *thieves*? Thieves? Going to the only guarded tomb in Jerusalem, when there were plenty of others they could have rifled, to rifle the tomb of the poorest man that had walked through those streets? When Jesus wanted to talk about a coin he had to say, 'Has anybody got a penny?' and they gave it to him from the crowd, and he held it up, had something to say, and then, presumably, gave it back. And he had the most interesting way of paying his taxes – but I will leave those of you with the same problem to find that one out![6]

'The poorest man in Jerusalem has just been buried, let us go and break the official seal and get to his tomb!' So the thieves risked their lives, and then left all the valuables behind. The graveclothes were neatly wrapped up together and left, and so were the costly spices. Nothing was taken except the body, and what can you do with that?

c. Could it then have been the *authorities* who removed the corpse, anticipating perhaps a bit of an uprising? 'Those Galileans are hot-headed, after too much drink on a festival occasion, they might, now that their leader has gone, start causing some trouble. Well, the best thing to do is to shift the body away from the shrine that they are bound to make out of the tomb; and then we will have the whole thing under control!'

Frankly, I think that would be the best way to start a

[6] See Matthew 17:27

riot, not to quell one. If they were hot-headed Galileans, to shift the body would be to them the last indignity to be given to their great leader. No, that was the very thing likely to cause a riot. Anyway, if for some other reason they removed the body from the tomb, surely it would have been the simplest thing in the world to have exposed the body when these men began to proclaim that Jesus was alive, and to have said, 'If anybody else goes around with this cock-and-bull story, they will look exactly the same as this corpse within a few days!'

They would have loved to have had the body somewhere, so that they could have produced it. For *they* were the ones accused; they had taken the Jewish Christ and executed him, as the apostles were proclaiming. If the authorities had stolen the body, why didn't they say so and produce it when the Christians were claiming Jesus had risen?

d. Even less probable is the suggestion that some lesser, *nondescript disciples* stole the body and deceived the leaders. But again, not a breath of such a suspicion ever existed in the early Christian community. Neither would the scepticism of a Thomas have been overcome by mere hearsay of lesser men. The same could also be said of the rest of the leadership. The leading apostles not only saw an empty tomb, but they also saw Jesus after the resurrection.

4. *Mistaken tomb theory*

Perhaps the tomb was a *mistaken* one – you know, early in the morning, Mary Magdalene, rather emotional, with lots of tears in her eyes. It's rather misty and she doesn't know Jerusalem; she goes to the wrong tomb, and there she meets a gardener. The gardener says, 'He is not here.' She thinks he said, 'He is risen.' She rushes back and tells Peter. Peter goes running out, and he finds the wrong tomb too, and so does John. Joseph of Arimathea then hears, and the tomb is in his own garden, but he also goes to the wrong one! And don't forget that the garden in which Jesus was buried would have been something like

Hampstead Heath on a Bank Holiday as soon as it started to get around that Jesus was risen! Nobody was going to believe that sort of story without putting their heads inside the sepulchre themselves, for everybody in Jerusalem knew it was being claimed that Jesus was alive. Surely not everybody in Jerusalem would find the wrong tomb and leave the right one, guarded, totally uninvestigated?

5. *Fainting theory*

Perhaps Christ only *fainted* on the cross and came round in the tomb when the cool air swept through. Being revived, he pushed the stone away in his physically wrecked condition – a stone which a bunch of women couldn't move – and appeared to his disciples, absolutely clapped out, with hands and feet bleeding, and his side marked from the spear thrust, and convinced them that he was the Prince of life who had conquered death. He then staggered out to let the whole hoax go on, and presumably to meet Paul on the Damascus Road, before disappearing into India or somewhere and from history.

This theory appears in a more sophisticated form in Dr Schonfield's book, *The Passover Plot*, where Jesus is depicted on the cover as a puppet with strings. In actual fact, says Schonfield, Jesus believed in the power of God, nevertheless he staged the whole crucifixion, because he believed sincerely that the Leader of Israel, the Messiah, must suffer according to the Scripture, but also return to reign. Well, we might ask, if he believed sincerely in the power of God, why did he have to play-act the crucifixion? God's power surely could be believed to cope with a resurrection as much as with anything else, especially if it were so certain that it was prophesied in the Scriptures.

Also, it might be asked why it was that only two minor disciples were in on this secret plan, *i.e.* to pretend he was dead and then to revive him so that he could reign, namely, Joseph of Arimathea and Nicodemus. Christ was supposed to have been drugged only, by the anodyne offered at the crucifixion, which the gospel writers say he refused. The fact was, says Schonfield, the plot failed because the soldier thrust his spear into Christ's side and really dealt a death blow. Schonfield, twenty centuries later, says that despite the spear wound, Jesus did come round in the tomb before he expired and sent messages to Peter, James and John via Joseph and Nicodemus, that they were to preach the good news in all the world. And that was sufficient to convince the apostles that he was alive! Such a glaring contradiction in the whole reconstruction of the story, that is, to say Jesus believed in God's power yet still felt he had to play-act at death, should surely have been avoided by such a close thinker as Dr Schonfield.

Besides the fact of the empty tomb, we have the claims of the first disciples that they *saw Jesus risen.* Some have ascribed this to hallucinations.

6. *Hallucination theory*

If the Lord Jesus did not faint, then was it perhaps possible that people had *hallucinations*, thinking that they saw him? You know women, they are a bit prone to these things; Mary of Magdalene, for instance, she was that type! They are very emotional. But it wasn't only women, it was hard-headed fishermen, tax-collectors (I wish my tax-collector would have a few hallucinations!). It was not just women by themselves, or men by themselves; it was bunches of people. It was not just in the morning, or in the afternoon, or in the evening; it was all times of the day.

Most people suffering from hallucinations find that if the visions die away, they do so gradually as time goes on, becoming less and less frequent. But these appearances of Jesus happened for forty days only and then they stopped suddenly for everybody. It was not likely to be hallucinations that gave rise to the resurrection story, and anyway they could not account for the empty tomb.

7. *Legends*

Of course the stories could be just *legends*, surely, one must allow that! There are legends that have grown up around all great men. Jesus was a great healer; he had done many miracles; surely legendary figures like this are bound to get stories attached to them. But the material we have hardly appears legendary. The apostle Paul tells us, having been converted within three to five years of the crucifixion, that he received this message, 'that Christ had died according to the Scriptures, and rose again.'[7] Three or even five years is not very long for some fanciful story to attach itself around a popular leader.

Moreover, if you read the New Testament, you don't find the atmosphere of legends: most of the writings are given in a factual way, within some thirty or forty years of the events. They are written as from eye-witnesses, and these eye-witnesses report, and their reports integrate, as men who have been in the event and seen these things.

If you were writing a legend, you could not have resisted more detail about the actual resurrection itself, could you? The shaking and the quivering of the body, that is bound to turn your readers on! The movement of the clothes, the upheaval in the tomb – you could not have left out all that! Yet not a word is said. Why? because nobody saw it. They wrote only what they saw. Peter and James had private interviews with Jesus after the resurrection. Would you not have liked to have heard what happened when Peter saw Jesus? 'Well, Peter, so you denied me, did you? I suppose you will need forgiveness . . . *etc.*' – you would love to have heard it all, and seen Peter really put in his place! Even more interesting would be a scene when Jesus confronted his unbelieving half-brother James. Not a word said about it, just that these interviews happened; we don't know, fortunately, the personal context. The bits that we would have loved if we were writing legends are just not there.

Added to this, what legend from the first century would say that the first apostle (meaning 'one who is sent') to the apostles was a woman? Mary Magdalene was sent, 'Go and tell my brothers.' You would not have let them get away with that, would you? First-century legends of that

[7] 1 Corinthians 15:1–8.

calibre would never have got off the ground when there was no Women's Lib. around.

These are the accounts. Nondescript disciples like Cleopas, on the road back from Emmaus, come back to Jerusalem and tell how they have met the Lord. Would legend record the unbelief of the big-time apostles, and Thomas in particular? I remember once in a university a fellow coming up to talk to me after a meeting, looking over my shoulder as I was reading a passage of the Bible. He said, 'Hey, this fellow Matthew is not trying to con us, is he? Look, he puts down here that when Jesus appeared, some of his disciples didn't believe in him.[8] If Matthew had been trying to con us he would not have put that in, would he?' We have got the factual accounts. They don't read like fairy stories, written up later as legends, but historical eyewitness documents.

The fact of the matter

Apart from the seven objections to the resurrection which we have dealt with above, there are seven positive points which add their reasonableness to the case for the resurrection.

1. *The Old Testament* said it would happen, foreshadowing it by men such as Isaac and Jonah received back from the dead, by its inference that the 'suffering servant' would reign as King for ever and ever, and by explicit prophecies concerning the resurrection of Christ in Psalms, Isaiah and Hosea.

2. *Christ* taught that it would happen, although his disciples record that they did not believe him. He said he must suffer many things at the hands of the leaders, and on the third day rise again.

3. *The disciples,* after the resurrection, believed, and said he did do it, and they would have taken more convincing than any.

4. *Sunday* became the day on which the Christians met

[8] Matthew 28:17.

to worship, whereas the sabbath as God's day had been written into the Jew for over 1200 years. It needed such a trauma as a rising from the dead to give the first day of the week a greater significance than the sabbath.

5. *The message* was 'Jesus is alive', not some abstract philosophical or theological concept. The disciples didn't preach 'God is love' and 'Love your neighbour' – at least, not at first – but that God had done something powerful in history. Yes, 'Jesus is alive.'

6. *Today* all over the world there are men and women who say: We have found that our experience that Christ is alive can be interpreted and attested only by this event in history. The two accord – the living Christ today in our lives and what happened in the history of mankind 2,000 years ago. The existence of the church is substantial evidence, for it is not a philosophical society of learning, or a religious club, but a community based on the assertion that Christ is risen.

7. *Eternal life* Above all those things, if Jesus really were who he claimed to be, God speaking to man in man's sufferings, and in man's death, if Jesus really were God, should we be surprised that this irresistible resurrecting God breaks out of the tomb we gave him and starts to show us he is alive? Eternal life has this kind of permanence. He does it when we try to bury him in our subconscious too. I remember one atheist looking almost neurotic and saying to me when I asked if he ever thought of God, 'I never *stop* thinking about God!' Of course, because God is alive in Christ seeking to make himself known.

In the resurrection God really did beat the grave. The apostle Paul sums it up like this: ' "Death is swallowed up in victory." "O death, where is thy victory? O death, where is thy sting?" The sting of death is sin, and the power of sin is the law. But thanks be to God, who gives us the victory through our Lord Jesus Christ."[9]

[9] 1 Corinthians 15:54–57.

Removing the sting

An Indian friend of mine tells how he saw a woman, devoted to her child, snatch it up when it had been bitten by a snake. She proceeded to bite, then suck the wound drawing the poison out and into herself. She died, but the child lived. Now the 'sting of death', that is its fear and pain, is sin. The strength of that sin is the law, that God condemns sin. We know we're sinners, and sin stings and bites into our beings. But Christ has sucked the sting, swallowed death, tasted death for every man.[10] He borrowed our death because he had no death on his own account; he borrowed mankind's death in order to suck it up, swallow it up, to finish with it so that we might live. He died that we might live.

A Christian in a Nazi concentration camp spoke to a Jewess about Jesus. She reacted, 'Jesus died for me but I don't understand it, I don't get it. How do you mean, Jesus died for me? It doesn't make sense.' One day she is in a queue of people with her towel over her arm, her number on it. She thinks she is going to the washrooms. Unknown to her, it is the gas chamber! The Christian sees her standing there. She senses the situation: that whole crowd of Jews is being deceived into death. She says, 'Excuse me, would you mind running back to the billet, I have left my soap there? I will hold your towel and your place.' When the Jewess came back the queue had moved in. The Christian woman had died in her place. That Jewess actually came out of the camp under the other woman's name and number. She had begun to understand how Christ had died for her.

I know a man who was, for a large part of his life, an atheist. He was a member of the Communist party, until Hungary was suppressed. Then he left the Communist party like many at that time on conscience grounds, saying, 'Whatever life is about it certainly cannot help mankind to act in these ways. I must look further.' He was a

[10] See Hebrews 2:9.

first-class scientist, a doctor of chemistry. Finding that most of his work was going into atomic war-heads, he left the research industry and became a school-teacher (his pay dropped, of course!). He was still an atheist and sought to follow what he knew as the truth.

One day he was asked by his headmaster to speak at school assembly. He answered to this effect: 'I'm sorry, Sir, but I haven't an ounce of religion in me.' 'Don't let that worry you,' the headmaster said, 'just tell them that science has made the universe so big that man therefore is so small he ought to be humble.' He agreed to have a go at it because, after all, he didn't want to lose another job! He tried to tell the school in that particular morning assembly that science had made the world and universe so big and man was so small, therefore he ought to be humble. He didn't think he had done too well (neither did anyone else!).

The following week a local minister came to the school; he himself had only recently made the astounding discovery that Jesus really is alive. He gave a good talk about being humble because Christ has beaten our biggest problem, death, and if we call him Lord, then we can begin to find the answer to other problems. But, of course, you have to be humble to call him Lord. The science teacher was very impressed with what he heard. Approaching the minister afterward, he said, 'Can you tell me any more about this? Have you anything more I can read about it?' The minister took from his pocket a little booklet called *The Evidence for the Resurrection*.[11]

That evening the teacher went through the pamphlet and decided that it was very cool, straightforward and plain, and as a scientist, since the facts seemed pretty strong, he ought to do something about it for it seemed to present a good case. That night he got his wife's Bible and began to read. He read on right through till the morning, then went to school and announced himself in the staff room as a Christian. The only evidence he could show them were the bags under his eyes – he had been up

[11] J. N. D. Anderson, *The Evidence for the Resurrection* (IVP, 1950).

all night! He went to the sixth form free-thinking club and told them he had become a Christian. They were a little non-plussed at this.

Two days later the school religious instruction master came to his home and said, 'We are very surprised that you have become a Christian after all these years; after all, we know your background and your atheism. I expect you don't really know much about Christianity?' He replied, 'No, I don't really, but do come in.' So the Scripture master explained all sorts of difficulties about being a Christian. After some of these difficulties, as he saw them, had been spelt out about the Bible and Christ, the science master replied: 'I'm very sorry, I haven't really followed much of what you have been saying, as I have only been a Christian two days, but one thing I do know is, *Jesus is alive, isn't he?*'

The living God

Jesus is alive, isn't he? Jesus' dying on the cross takes the sting out of death because it deals with the problem of sin itself, yours and mine, that we might begin to discover in our experience a *living God – a God who is alive*, as alive as a man who has burst forth out of the grave. It is that Christ who is the Christ of Christianity.

In the last book of the Bible, Jesus is depicted as standing at the door of our lives, knocking. We feel this knocking when we sense that we should respond to God. When we know that God is saying something to us, then he knocks. 'Behold, I stand at the door and knock; if any one hears my voice and opens the door, I will come in to him and eat with him': I will live with that person.[12] This is the offer and the promise of the living Lord Jesus to any who begin to sense that there is a knocking at their lives.

Perhaps God has been knocking for some while. We have ignored it; we have not faced up to whose hand is knocking. It is the hand of God revealed in Christ, asking us to respond by the exposure of our lives to him, saying,

[12] Revelation 3:20.

'Please come in; take over; begin to deal with me in a living way, not only to meet the problem of death, but the problem of life itself, the problem of my need and my sin. Please come in.'

'Behold, I stand at the door and knock; if any one hears my voice and opens the door, I will come in' – It is a promise, *I will*, full of power, for he is *alive*!

7
The beautiful people

We make a very significant step forward in getting involved with God when we come to realize that God is not very interested in nice people – well, no more interested in them than in anyone else. It is emancipating to discover that God's interest is in men and women just as they are and wherever they are. He is not particularly partial to those who might have been fortunate enough to have had a nice background, balanced upbringing, plenty of good inheritance genes so that they can swing into life on all cylinders and be psychologically very well forward in the *avant garde* of human advance.

Thank God he is not interested only in them, for the majority of the human race is not like that. Most of mankind have been somewhat battered in their psychology, have had shattering traumas when children, have been smashed in life through suffering or their bodies have been racked with pain. They have been brought up with views of life which nurtured strange ideas and cramped their minds – that is, if they have ever had the energy to think at all, having had less than enough to eat. Some men and women have inherited all sorts of disadvantages which nice people never have, and so have had to hassle with all sorts of quirks and eccentricities in their sex life, struggling to be the sort of decent people that at times they felt they wanted to be. Others have felt the great passions that they have inherited in the chemicals of their make-up, and have not been able to overcome them in moments of stress. And others, lacking any nice things, have crept their way through life with all sorts of inhibitions, psychological disorders, disadvantages of education, health, wealth. So, thank God he is not just interested in nice people! If you happen to be a 'nice' type, then you are fortunate – that is what it amounts to really – because the majority of people just haven't got that head start in life.

One day a man came to Jesus Christ who really was very 'nice' indeed.[1] He was a rich man, and that usually helps you to be nice. He was in government too, and of course having influence over others is always handy to keep you on a well-balanced keel. He had been well brought up, so much so that Jesus virtually commended him that he had not lied, and he didn't oppress others, he was not a murderer, he didn't steal, he wasn't the sort of man who would break the basic laws of morality. None-theless, the man knew that there was something missing and asked: 'What must I do to inherit eternal life?'

Now, of course, eternal life is that life that belongs to God, so to possess it means getting involved with God. But how do I get involved with God? Jesus' reply was: 'Sell what you have and come, follow me.' 'Get involved with me,' says Jesus, for Christ is eternal life, and Christ is what God is doing in this world. Christ is God's own eternal life pumped into humanity to get them moving in his stream of things. So, the reply of Jesus was: 'Get rid of what you have inherited; get rid of your past back-log; get rid of your advantages and privileges; forget your hereditary genes which have served you so well, and pitch everything into a total, new abandonment to the life of God. Come, follow me.' The young man was a 'nice' person, but Jesus was not too interested in that. His call

[1] Luke 18:18–25.

to and for all men is 'Ditch the riches of your psychology, your mentality, your past, and come. Come just as you are, poor, in need, spiritually bankrupt, and get involved with what Jesus Christ is offering you, eternal life.'

Jesus told a story about two fellows, one of whom was very religious.[2] They went up to the temple to pray, and the religious one said: 'Thank you, God, that I give you a tenth of everything that I have and that I even fast, denying myself for others. I thank you that I am not an extortioner. – I'm a very good employer; you go and ask my friends! I don't cheat people. I have never murdered. I have never stolen, and I have kept the commandments quite well really!' Then he looked sideways, and to his disgust found that somebody else had crept in to the religious meeting in the temple. It was one of those nasty, corrupt types who was a quisling, sold out to the foreign government that was in power, and making quite a good racket out of it too – a tax-collector! And this man in the corner was beating his chest and crying: 'O God, be merciful to me; I am bankrupt as far as you are concerned!' So, looking across at him, and then quickly away again of course, the first man, the Pharisee, continued to pray: 'I thank you, God, that I am not like that tax-collector!' 'After all,' he implied, 'You must be very pleased to have a friend as good as me when characters like that are around!'

Such a nice person!

The Pharisee was a nice chap. He himself was certain of it and others doubtless thought so too. He was the sort of fellow you like to work for. I like to work for somebody who does not use extortion and oppress me, don't you? I like a fellow who is not an adulterer, especially if my daughter is around, don't you? And I certainly like somebody who is going to pay 100 pence to the pound and fork out a bit for charity occasionally. The Pharisee was

[2] Luke 18:9–14.

all this and told God so in his prayer, in case the Almighty had forgotten. But you see, Jesus was not too interested in the nice person as such; he seemed more interested in the wretch who was beating his chest and saying: 'There are all sorts of ugly, filthy, twisted things inside me, and I need help.' That is the man who got involved with God. For Jesus said: 'He went down to his house right, right with God', which means not only *right* with him, but right *with* him, and involved with him. He can do something with a man like that in this world.

In the final analysis, when a man is stripped of all his psychological advantages and stands as a naked soul before God, then we see the real man. When the soul stands naked before God, the final, fundamental decisions of the spirit will be revealed – the things that we really chose; the things that we really ached for and wanted to be; the decisions we made about life but did not find the power to effect. This is the real final man that lies inside and which will stand before God. It is in this that God is interested. At that final time we will have sloughed off all that we, happily perhaps, or maybe unhappily, happened to inherit as our psychological backlog.

That is why you can point at so many Christians and say, 'They are not particularly "nice" people.' No, not yet. They have a long way to go; they started with a lot of disadvantages and lack of privileges. And that is why you can look at some non-Christians and think, 'They are very, very nice folk.' Yes, they are swinging into life quite well. But they would be a lot different again if they came to the point of acknowledging that they need something else, something which God calls eternal life – his life, which means getting involved with him. He showed us how it could be because he put that life in Christ, when Christ came to this world. He revealed eternal life as a man, so that we men could get involved with God. His life then becomes the very power and the pulse of our being and moves us out into the world in God's way and in God's movement.

Simply perfect

All this is not to say, of course, that a Christian is not to become – well, something better than 'nice'. Ultimately God is concerned to make us perfect. 'Be perfect, as your heavenly Father is perfect.' 'He sends rain on the just and on the unjust'[3] – perfect towards all men. Christ has set himself that task. When the rich young ruler came to him, Jesus said: 'If you want to be perfect, you lack one thing. Get rid of your inheritance and come, follow me – we will do things together.'[4] It is perfection that God is after, not nice people. We may take a long while getting there, but that is what he wants.

But perhaps we are not prepared to let God so deal with us that we become perfect men and women, because we don't really like the idea of becoming perfect. We don't mind the idea of being nice; everyone will say: 'They are beautiful people; they are lovely people!' But to become perfect, that is a different matter altogether. That means putting your hands into the trouble. It means getting a bit stained with suffering. It means getting involved with sacrifice and self-denial. I'm not quite sure that I'm willing for that sort of call. 'Come, be perfect – as your heavenly Father is perfect.'

C. S. Lewis likens it to when you have toothache as a child: you go to bed and bite the tooth and hope that the pain will go. You know that if you went to Mum she would give you an aspirin and it would be all right, but then, next morning, there would be more treatment to follow – you would be packed off to the dentist, and he would start tinkering around with all the other teeth, and they would all start to ache, even those that hadn't ached before! Then there is the drill! Consequently, you don't tell Mum. You try to put up with the little inconvenience and make it slightly less painful, because you know you would get the whole works if you got involved with Mother, and the dentist too.

There is the same problem with Jesus Christ. When we

[3] Matthew 5:48 and 45.   [4] See Luke 18:22.

get involved with him, it is the whole works that he is committed to – this perfection which he is working towards. Not just tinkering around with the odd tooth, but a thorough examination; then the removal of the corruption, and the packing back in of something else which is going to make us able to bite hard into life. He is going to make us perfect, because there really is a perfect world that is going to come. Jesus promised it and even said that it was 'at hand'[5] – just around the corner.

It is God's kingdom, the kingdom of righteousness, justice, peace, love. It is for this kingdom men are being prepared and trained. That is the kingdom to which we are moving if we are involved with the life of God. And that is the kingdom for which we have to be prepared, by becoming perfect ourselves, by getting hold of this perfect life that Christ is offering.

This is what a Christian is. He is somebody who is in the movement of what God is doing through this world, moving towards his perfection. He is one who has received God's own life into himself and is in tune with the sphere of existence which God is going to bring on earth. The Christian lays hold of the values that belong to that kingdom even now, and starts to express them even before the final revolution comes. Although there may not be very many nice Christians around yet, when the life of Christ which has got inside them has done its full work, when they have been stripped of all their inherent selfishness which they will be only too pleased to shed, just to look at them will make you want to fall down and worship. Just to look at them will make you want to say: 'What a magnificent thing!' Yes, that is what God is doing. A new kingdom will be born and there will be men who have been born for it because they have God's own life.

Getting started

Now as we have been thinking of the implications of the Christian faith, no doubt some of you have been beginning

[5] Matthew 4:17.

to say: 'Well, how can this particular encounter that you talk about, this getting involved with God, this being wrapped up with his life and with his person, how can this actually happen to me? How can I be involved with this movement of God, this "perfection trip" if you like? How can a person begin to know God?'

There are three ways (which can sometimes be three difficulties) that I want to highlight, for there are many who want to know how such an encounter with Jesus Christ really can take place in their experience.

1. *Knowing*

If I meet somebody I might say: 'I know that man', because I have met him. But how can I say I know God, or for that matter, how can I say I know anything? There are three factors involved:

a. We can know something because *an authority* has told us. He has given us his testimony, and we believe his authority.

b. Another way is to use *our reason*. We think as hard as we can until we say: 'Now I know – it is reasonable; I have reasoned it out.'

c. We can know by *experience*; *e.g.* I know that there are animals that carry babies around in their pockets because I have been to Australia and I've seen such creatures!

These three ways usually interplay upon each other in order to help us to *know* something; for example, when you were a child your mother told you not to put your fingers in the fire or they would get burned. Furthermore she put a guard round the fire to make quite sure you couldn't experiment. You had to accept Mother's *authority* on the matter; after all, mothers are right about most things. Besides, as you grew older and more observant, you noticed that things that were put on the fire usually went up in smoke! *Reason* told you it was probable that fire could burn fingers also. The day came however when you stumbled near an unguarded fire, put your hand out to save yourself and . . . *experience* confirmed your mother's authority and your own reasoning in an unforgettable way. You really know now about fire burning fingers.

Similarly, when you become a Christian, you have usually considered the *authority* of God's Word and the testimony of other Christians; you may be convinced by your *reason* that God exists and is worth knowing, that you are a rebel cut off from God's life, needing forgiveness; that Jesus died to make possible your recovery and restoration and offers you his risen life. Now comes the moment when you have to use *experience*. So you pray; you admit your need; you ask for forgiveness and a new relationship with God; you commit yourself.

You may not immediately experience anything much, but sense dictates that you persevere and see that the conditions are right; you approach God humbly and willing to do his will, prepared to forgive and love all men, ready to make changes and most of all to make God the most important thing in your life, to spend time *getting to know* him. The ensuing days begin to demonstrate to you that the authority you followed was right, and your reason was right: now your experience confirms it and you can say, 'I *know*.' His life has begun to work in you.

So if you are saying to yourself, 'How can I know that I am a Christian?', 'How can I really know that God has given me this eternal life?' then you have, perhaps, reached this step of knowing by experience. You have thought hard about the Christian faith; now comes the point where you must offer yourself personally to God.

2. *Seeing*

But there is another way we can talk about this encounter. Sometimes we say, 'Oh, I *see* now.' Maybe I have been looking at what it means to be a Christian; I have been examining the claims; I have been thinking hard: but somehow or other, it just does not seem to come alive to me.

Imagine yourself in a hut in a garden. You shut the door and it is pitch black except for one beam of light coming through a crack in the shed wall. You look at the beam of light – you can measure it, you can perhaps ascertain its intensity; you can see some other things by it, as you put them in its path. In that way you stand apart and examine the whole thing objectively. But there comes a moment, as you move across the hut from one position to another, when you stand in that beam of light that is pouring in, and you look along it, upwards, out into the fuller light, and see the trees, the birds, the clouds, the sky, and then the sun, millions of miles away. A whole new world opens up and you now say, 'I know that light in another way from the way I knew it when I measured it and determined its intensity.' You have changed your position and it has become something experimental.

To know a person, too, one has to reach that particular stage. It means more than facts and figures – age, sex, height and colour of hair. It means spending time with that person and discovering what they think, how they react, what they value most highly. It also means seeing *ourselves* as the other person sees us – and that is sometimes an unpleasant surprise! It means, without in any sense changing the person we are, at the same time being able to put ourselves in their shoes, think their thoughts, see things with their perspective, react as they would react. Any deep relationship involves becoming *like* the other person in this way, at least to some degree.

And this is what it means to become a Christian. We get involved with God. We put ourselves in his searching light and admit our failures and need. We feel the warming light of his promised forgiveness and new life. We spend time listening to what he has to say in the words specially preserved for us in the Bible. Here we see more of God and more of ourselves. We speak to him (what we usually call praying) and are ready for what he may want to say to us, too. Standing in the light he has provided for us, we can look out on the world and really see it, for the first time, with his perspective. And we will see a whole new life coming into view.

This life is also seen in others. It was perfectly expressed in Jesus who was the 'living image' of God. But as Christ lives in other believers we see in them the fulfilment of God's design when he made man in his own image. And thus we see God in other people. Our Christian life becomes a further knowing of him in the fellowship of his people.

3. *Believing*

Thirdly, perhaps some of you say, 'But I haven't got enough faith. You have to have faith to become a Christian, and I haven't got it!' Well, it is true, if you are going to have a relationship with *anybody* you have to have a certain amount of faith: faith that the look on their face is to some degree a true reflection of what is going on inside; faith that the words they use are a genuine expression, to some extent, of what they want to say. To meet God too you have to have a certain amount of faith. But with many of us our trouble is this, instead of majoring on the little bit of faith that is always necessary for a relationship, we major on the doubts, and we build on them. So we never find this relationship.

Consider what would happen if I did this with my wife. Suppose I arrived home after some days of work away, and on my way I met a 'friend' who said, 'Hey, Rog, you've been away for some time, haven't you? Well, a lot of funny people have been going in and out of your house. I don't know who your wife has around there when you're not at home!' As I listen to what he says I could do one of two things: I could either begin to doubt my wife's integrity, or I could be sensible and say to myself, 'Well, everything I know about my wife is trustworthy. She gives herself sacrificially for the children and me. She is always, to my knowledge, very loving and faithful . . . that is what I know about her. So I'm going to major on that.' In that case I would brush off the doubt that might have been planted in my mind and would go into my home saying, 'How've you been getting on while I've been away, my dear? I hope everything has gone well?' And straightaway we have set up a loving, trusting relationship again. But suppose I went in saying, 'Now what's all this I've been hearing about you?', then I am unlikely to be able to build a relationship with her.

Similarly I cannot encounter and begin a relationship with God unless I use the little bit of faith I have already to build on. I have to major on the fact that there is enough evidence to demonstrate that God is more likely to be there than he is not; and that there is sufficient indication to suggest that the claims of Jesus Christ are reasonable. If I thus begin to move in faith, in prayer, in that direction, and give myself to God, trusting what I know, then doubts will gradually be replaced by knowledge, and I will have a faith that gets bigger and bigger. To get off the ground in trusting God you have to take that small bit of knowledge of him and use it; so your faith will grow every day, and you will get stronger and stronger in the reality of the God who is getting involved with you. Facts are to be used in faith when building a relationship. All stable relationships require faith built on facts, and sensible people do not major on doubtful speculations

A whole new ball game

When a person gets involved with God and receives from him forgiveness and new life, three things, amongst others, begin to take place – three things that will drive us out into the world with a wholly different attitude.

1. *New life*

The first thing that happens is that *we find that God's life in us*, through that encounter with Jesus Christ, brings us to a *purpose*. It is not always a purpose that we can spell out exactly at the very beginning of our Christian experience, but like all life, we know it has a direction. The life in a frog's egg aims at producing a frog. Even though the jelly-enveloped egg initially releases a tadpole, because of the genetic information in each cell it will fulfil its destiny and become a frog. The life that was in the embryo in your mother's womb has now moved out into what we see in you today. There is a direction and a purpose in life. And God's life has a purpose. We sense that purpose even though we, as Christians, may not be able to define fully where it is going.

I hinted at what this purpose is at the very beginning of the chapter. It is to make us perfect, or perhaps more fully, it is to make us sons of God, patterned after his own Son. God did not choose that we should become supersonic angels; nor, from the beginning of time, did he choose that we should become high-powered psychedelic beasts. God's purpose, from the foundation of the world, is that we should take on the character, life, wisdom, purpose, communion, business and family life of God himself, by becoming sons of God. This will involve us in being 'men for others', as Christ was *par excellence*, and serving God's interests by serving our fellow-men as Christ did, being called a servant and saying himself that he came to serve and not to be served.

When I become a Christian and receive that life of God, I begin to find God's purpose pulsating through my being to make me like his Son; to make me love like his Son, bear suffering as his Son, to live sacrificially like his Son, to carry the mercy of God to others as his Son carries it . . . and so on. Even more, a son can look into his Father's face and say 'Father', and get to know him. That is the over-all purpose which God brings into our experience when we become Christians.

Of course, this major eternal purpose will have its reflection in some subsidiary purposes – micro-affairs connected with this temporal life. One Christian is going to have an adventure with God in the academic world; another in the engineering department; another in agriculture, in music, or entertainment, or business: there are a thousand and one things in which to be involved with the life of God; situations in which God is wanting to involve himself and get working with us.

I don't know what your adventure will be. God has different ones for different people, in different places and at different times. Each is the particular exploit best suited to the person you are, the work he wants to do with you, and the people he wants to involve you with. To be in a life with God is absolutely unlimited in its possibilities. We must expose ourselves and be available for that encounter, so that he may take over and start to share eternal life with us.

2. *New power*

The second great thing that happens is that *we discover a new power.* All of us at times must have known: 'I cannot do the good I want, but the evil I do not want is what I do.'[6] This is our bankruptcy. This is the failure of our poverty. It comes partly from the kick-back of the environment into which we have been pitched, partly from the heredity that we have gained from the human race. The result is, 'I cannot do the good I want, but the evil I do not want is what I do.' The eternal life of God brings a power to work within us so that step by step, assuredly and significantly, we begin to embrace our failure and overcome it. We have a new power.

I remember some years ago a young fellow phoned me late one night. I was reluctant to talk with him because I knew all about his problem and my previous attempts to advise him had been fruitless. He had been treating his wife very badly; he had been unfaithful to her many times and seemed incapable of seeing how deeply he was hurting her. Now finally she was leaving him and he was faced with the prospect of divorce, which he did not really want. His latest 'affair' was with a girl involved in occult practices and she seemed to have such a hold on him that he was unable to end the relationship. So now he was desperate, pleading for help. 'You've got to help me somehow; my whole life will break up. I don't want to lose my little boy, I really do love him. I've not cared so much about my wife, it's true, but I got my job through my father-in-law and I'll lose that too if I'm not careful!' He really was worried about himself. So he drove the few

[6] Romans 7:19.

miles to my house and rang the doorbell. Just then, by a remarkable coincidence, his wife walked up the path. She had felt equally desperate and had come to see if my wife could help her. She had come by train, he by car, and they had quite unexpectedly met on the doorstep! We hastily parted them.

I began to talk to the fellow. His whole attitude was selfish and egocentric; he was concerned with what he was going to lose, how he was suffering, what it meant to him, with no thought of what he was doing to his wife. After a couple of hours of this I asked him, 'Are you prepared to talk to God about it?' To my surprise he answered, 'Yes, I will.' And he started to pray.

When you pray in this kind of situation, you realize it is useless to try to 'con' God. You have to be honest and real. I had read him verses from the New Testament that urge 'Husbands, love your wives'[7] – with no ifs or buts! So he confessed honestly, 'God, I have never loved my wife. Please forgive me. And will you help me?' That was the most sincere thing he had said all evening! We both prayed on our knees, then sat down again. Suddenly God's power began to come upon him and he started to shake, then to cry. To see a strong man cry is always rather overwhelming, so I got him on his knees again and he wept as he poured out his heart to God and found forgiveness of sins. At last we sat back again in our chairs and he said to me, 'Roger, I've never felt so clean in all my life.' Then he added, 'You know, I saw the Lord.' 'What do you mean, you saw the Lord?' 'Well,' he said, 'I saw him high and lifted up. I didn't see his face or anything but I just knew that he was lifted up above all this situation.' Now those were his exact words.

At this point I thought it was about time to bring in his wife. My wife and I left them, since there was a touching reconciliation scene between the two. I asked my wife, 'How did you get on with her?' She replied, 'Well, I felt she was having the rough side of the situation, so I was

[7] Ephesians 5:28.

praying that God would give me something to help her. And he gave me Isaiah chapter 6. So I read from the sixth chapter of Isaiah and said to her, "We must pray for your husband that he *sees the Lord*, because he does not feel his sin." ' I was amazed and said to my wife, 'Do you know what he has just said to me?', and I told her. Now this is how Isaiah chapter 6 reads:

'In the year that King Uzziah died I saw the Lord . . . high and lifted up; and his train filled the temple . . . and the house was filled with smoke' (speaking of the mysterious presence of God). The doorposts shook at his presence and the seraphim cried, 'Holy, holy, holy is the Lord of hosts; the whole earth is full of his glory.' Isaiah then cried out and said, 'I am a man of unclean lips, and I dwell in the midst of a people of unclean lips; for my eyes have seen the King, the Lord of hosts!' And a coal was taken from the altar (a picture of the place of sacrifice where Christ, the great sacrifice of God himself was offered up for the world) and it was laid on Isaiah's lips and his sin was purged. That was Isaiah's experience thousands of years ago, and that night it had been the experience of this young man. 'I have never felt so clean in all my life,' he had said. 'I saw the Lord high and lifted up above all this situation.'

Six months later I took him with me to a meeting some miles away. On the way home, he said, 'Oh Rog, can't you put your foot down on that accelerator? This is the longest I have been away from my wife since we came to your house that night, and I'm really missing her. You know, I was a fool to look at any other woman. My wife has been such a help to me. You'd never believe what a wonderful life we have together now as we help each other in knowing God!' He had found a *power* in God to make a new man of himself. Hardly surprising that he makes his first aim now the business of Jesus Christ

3. *New love*

Thirdly, *there is a passion which eternal life brings* when we welcome Christ into our lives, a passion for God which overspills in love for others. I remember taking some meetings in a university where there was a fellow who went to his room after one of the meetings and, desiring to do God's will, simply asked Jesus Christ to come and take over his life. The following weekend we went to his home in an area where there lived many Asian immigrants. He had been brought up to hate immigrants. His father's job depended on there not being too many immigrants, or so he was led to believe. Anyway, they were different and lived differently. John had been brought up to hate what seemed to threaten his privileged position.

As he walked down the street that Saturday morning, he saw an Asian coming along on the other side of the road. Suddenly he was surprised at himself, he was aware that something had changed in him. The man who, a few days before, had spoken words to the effect, 'All right, God, I want to start going your way, will you get involved with me?', found that he was looking at that Pakistani with a love which he had not known before. He had a new outlook which later on took him into the immigrant scene with a desire to share Jesus Christ, and to work for those who have come as strangers to this country and are seeking to find a proper place in it.

The love of God overspills when we let it into our lives. It gives us the motivation, not for far-distant scenes about which we can only dream, but for the immediate scene and wherever God will ultimately place us in this world, to meet the real needs of men and women – to be loved, and to discover reality, and to be involved in God's movement – making *real* people for his kingdom.

Close encounter

But this will happen only when we come to God and admit that, though we may like to pretend to be 'beautiful people', our lives are really rather ugly. And you and I find it so hard to come and stand before God and say, 'I need you. I am bankrupt, but I want this life that you offer.' We find it so hard to repent and say, 'I'm sorry.'

This is the problem. Only good men have the humility to say they are sorry and repent, but it is only bad men that need to repent. It is so humbling to say you are sorry, that you were wrong, and that you need help. It takes more humility that most of us have. Perhaps that is one of the many things that Jesus Christ did for us when he died on the cross. Because he was a good man and had nothing to repent of, he was able to go through a repentance for us, to experience the humiliation of being sorry and repenting, of hanging his head in shame, and saying, 'My God, my God, why . . .?' As a good man, he could do it; he could humble himself to that degree, so that when we come fumblingly to God, trying to do it, he is there to help us. It's just like a child trying to write letters. He makes a scrawl, until Father puts his hand over the child's hand and, because he has the ability, does it perfectly for and with the child.

Perhaps you are saying you do not feel sorry enough; perhaps you don't feel bad enough. Maybe you never will, but you still have to repent. If you come just as you are, Jesus Christ will help you because he knows exactly what you are going to go through and what he has been through, and he puts his hand over yours and helps you to say, 'I'm sorry. I'm only fit for the crucifixion that Jesus had, only fit to be written off as waste. I certainly have not got in me the ability to take up my cross daily and follow him, the life-style that he calls me to. But I believe that if he comes with me I will have a new life and a new power. Please come into my life, Lord Jesus Christ, and start this eternal life of God in me.'

Then you have started on the process which God intends for every man and woman – life with a purpose, with a new power and with a love for God. It is possible really to love God! And as you begin to love him you will find that beauty, that love in you overspilling to other people.

8

In the end . . . God

'Then Death and Hades were thrown into the lake of fire. This is the second death . . . and if any one's name was not found written in the book of life, he was thrown into the lake of fire. Then I saw a new heaven and a new earth.'[1]

At the very beginning of his preaching, Jesus declared, 'The kingdom is at hand', implying that a man should put out his hand and start to take it: that kingdom in which there dwells love and righteousness, justice, peace, truth, beauty and goodness. His kingdom is the kingdom of those values which all seem to go down into the dust in man's death and seem to be ignored in life by many who are the great and mighty of this world. We all tend to live as though a kingdom of such values never did or could or would exist. But Jesus says that kingdom does exist and will come. The world scene will not always be 'As it was in the beginning, so it shall be ever more'.

'In the beginning God . . .' says the first page of the Bible. And 'in the end God . . .' we might infer from the last pages of Jesus' message. 'In the beginning God . . .' – he began it all. And 'in the end God' – he will finish it also, with the golden age of man's full development and fruition, the age which burns in all men's breasts, the hope for mankind. A future utopia, a golden age, taken by sleight of hand from Christianity by envious atheistic humanists who look forward to progressive technology launching us into a marvellous scientific euphoria of the future.

The hope is there; it is always there; it has always been there, until, perhaps, the twentieth century, when the

[1] Revelation 20:14–5; 21:1

rumblings and the labour pains of this kingdom have so shaken mankind that maybe the woman that is seeking to bring to birth will herself go down into death before the child is born.[2] Indeed, the pains of man's suffering, of inhumanity, of war upon war, and a never-ending stream of blood, seem rather to signal that mankind has no hope and that these dreams can never find fulfilment. Nevertheless, the Christian says, in the beginning God, and in the end, not man and his great kingdom but God himself will intervene.

This is what Jesus meant by saying that he was going to come again. That hope will be realized, but it will be realized in God's way in God's world, not in man's way in God's world – which is only hastening on at tremendous speed a dead end, the annihilation of our human race.

'Who are you?' said the prime minister, opening the door. 'I am God,' replied the stranger. 'I don't believe you,' said the prime minister, 'show me a miracle!' And God showed him the miracle of birth. 'Oh, that is nothing,' said the prime minister, 'my scientists are creating life in test-tubes and have nearly solved the secret of heredity. Artificial insemination is more certain than your lackadaisical methods, and by cross-breeding we are producing fish and mammals to our own design. Show me a proper miracle.' God caused the sky to darken and hailstones came pouring down. The prime minister picked up his phone to the Air Ministry: 'Send me a Met plane and sprinkle the clouds with silver iodide crystals, will you, old man?' The Met plane went up and sprinkled the clouds which had darkened the sky, and the hailstones stopped coming down and the sun shone. 'Show me another.' And God caused a plague of frogs to descend upon the land. The prime minister picked up his phone: 'Get the Ministry of Agriculture and Fisheries,' he said to the operator, 'and get them to prepare a frog killer, as myxomatosis killed rabbits.' Soon the land was free from frogs and the people gave thanks to the prime minister and erected laboratories in his name! 'Show me another.' God caused the sea to divide. The prime minister picked up his telephone to the Polaris submarine: 'Drop

[2] Matthew 24:8–14

a few ICBMs into the Antarctic and melt the ice cap, will you, old man?' The ice cap melted into water and the sea came rushing back. 'I will kill all the firstborn,' said God. 'Paltry trick,' said the prime minister. 'Watch this!' He pressed the button on his desk, and missiles flew to their pre-ordained destinations and H-bombs split the world asunder, and radio-activity killed every mortal thing. 'I can raise the dead,' said God. 'Please, please,' said the prime minister from his cardboard coffin, 'let me live again.' 'Why? Who are you? Who are you?' said God, closing the lid. . .
Anon.

In the end . . . God. If God does not have the last word the last word will be a very, very last word of emptiness and nothingness, fulfilling all the fears of the human heart that is emptied of the presence of its Creator.

Future shock

Jesus Christ had much to say concerning the end of time, the judgment of God and the kingdom that he was to inaugurate, in which the true values of men and women would persist for eternity. These would be brought to focus in his coming again to this earthly scene, to wind up the affairs of men. Christians call it his 'second coming'.

The New Testament speaks in almost every thirteenth verse of a kingdom that one day will be born, and the judgment which will usher it in, and the coming of the King who will establish it. Because it is a future event it is easy, of course, to dismiss the reality of such words as these which Jesus spoke. If, however, we have found something of the touch of his resurrection, if we have found the profundity of his crucifixion, stirring our souls, exposing our sin and meeting our deepest need; if we have faced the issue of his ethics and noticed how they transform men by challenging them to become new men; if we have felt the magnetism of his claim 'Come, follow me', and have tested the validity in this human scene of these appeals, finding them true: then, of course, we are going to take seriously what Jesus Christ had to say about the future.

There have been those, their ingenuity far exceeding their apparent scriptural knowledge, who have claimed to have discovered that the Bible says some interesting things about the Common Market, Napoleon, Mussolini and other figures that have arisen on the stage of history. I have even been informed by some extremely serious-faced 'prophets' that the great last 'world system' prophesied in the Bible is the Co-operative Society! No doubt a great deal of mis-use has been made of the statements that Jesus gave concerning his return and the wind-up of the age. No doubt a great deal of imagination has gone into those simple parables which were not meant to give us clues concerning the idiosyncracies and details of the end of this age of mankind, but rather were meant to impress us with the fact itself, for since this event has never happened, it is difficult to find language to describe it. Consequently, using imagery, likenesses and similes, Jesus puts over to us the fact that the end will come, time will be wound up, his kingdom will dawn, and he will reign. The symbols the Bible contains are to convey something of the triumph and majesty of the ways of God and that kingdom of love which will break into time and space. Jesus said he would come again, and his kingdom would be here.

Possibly

As we look at the facts, the *possibility* of the end of our age and the human race is certainly very much before us, insistently and persistently. I hope you don't think that I am being sensational or dramatic. If you have thought even a little concerning the stage at which the human race has arrived, you will very easily relate to me as I make some statements concerning the situation of man in the twentieth century.

The apocalyptic 'horsemen of war', famine and death, have been neighing at our gates, stamping their feet over a large part of our humanity for the last few years. Never has there been such bloodshed as has been seen in the twentieth century: 100,000,000 slaughtered in wars covering forty years, and millions described by Solzhenitsyn as passing through the Russian 'sewage disposal' system in the same time. Since World War II, more than forty wars have been declared. The only solution to famine posited by some politicians is that a vast amount of the human race must die, and then (romantically enough) America and Russia, as the two large powers, will become so selfless, they will supply the rest of mankind from their vast resources. But only after a vast proportion has died. Roughly one half of the world's population goes to bed hungry each night; the world has never known such famine conditions. Bangladesh and Ethiopia have given recent evidence that pestilence and disease are still a nemesis upon the human race.

And if we have looked to those traditional ways in which mankind has been threatened, and is being threatened on such a vast scale today, we might just for a moment think of the more recent ogre, the population explosion, which seems to be worsening the effects all round. Population numerics prophesied by our mathematicians have been exceeded again and again in the last few years. Certainly there is no indication of a run-down. Fred Hoyle has suggested that by the year 2250, when there could be 20–25 billion people in this world, there will just have to be one great slaughter to remove all but some two billion who can start again, if the human species is to have any possibility of continuance.[3]

We are on the threshold of one of the most incredibly traumatic times that mankind has ever gone through . . . if we get to the year 2250! Many academics raise these issues until they are sick of hearing their own bleat coming through the media, and we too would rather hide from the sombre facts they bring. It seems pretty certain with the rate of decrease in sea life that, if we continue in our present scheme, by the year 2000 it will be virtually extinct. Since 70% of our oxygen comes from sea life it does not bode well as to how much oxygen will be left for the human race. So presumably we won't have to

[3] Quoted by G. R. Taylor in *The Doomsday Book* (Thames and Hudson, 1970).

worry over much about the population increase!

The scientists could, of course, get to work on a bit of genetic engineering to produce some monstrosities of the human foetus that could better survive. The trouble is that you never know what liberties might be taken with the human brain and body; we are already pretty good at disposing of a large part of the human race (by abortion), without so much as a 'by your leave'. Perhaps we could pervert and twist some into new-type creatures? But a society made up of a scientist's dream of what man should or could be is enough to fill most of us with horror.

If we can't control the scientists, time itself is such a threat. Koestler, the great Hungarian thinker, has put it very, very poignantly: 'Time is running out. Nature has let us down, and it seems that God has left the phone off the hook.' What is man going to do? Even if somebody did bring something out of the scientific bag which could solve our problems, time would hardly be enough to implement it. Were there time enough before we were all extinguished, do you really think that the world as we know it, with its vested self-interest, would ever implement any major world-wide, hopeful, humanitarian solution? I hardly think so; even though there are idealistic dreamers, self-interest is too ingrained into our whole system, and changing the system does not change the men in whom self-interest is ingrained.

The tick of the clock

We have lost our nerve. We are all afraid, deep down. In 1955 Einstein and Russell got together; they were afraid. They said, 'Those who know the most are the most frightened men in our generation,' and they made a plea concerning the nuclear threat. So 1955 saw the birth of what we might call the 'bomb culture' (as Jeff Nuttal named it) whereby it seemed that no young people would talk about the future, because the future was so unsure; and all we could say about the present was that it was measured in the ticks of the bomb, as we waited for some great holocaust to blast off. Now that time has passed over the initial shock, we have repressed this sense deep down into our subconscious. Consequently we have a visionless, purposeless society, with some men and women who have stopped for a moment to think, or waited a moment to feel the subconscious pressure, then sung, painted and written of the total emptiness of our society and its impending doom. What has the Christian to say in such a situation, in this real world in which we live today?

Jesus told a story about his kingdom and its coming. He said it was something like bridesmaids waiting for the bridegroom and the bride to come and get on with the wedding feast.[4] But time dragged on (as some ladies are rather late to the altar). They went to sleep. Five of them slept and they were foolish; five of them slept and they were wise. When the cry went up, 'Behold, the bridegroom comes!', the wise arose and trimmed their lamps, and off they went through the night (as is the custom in the East) to the wedding feast. But the five foolish were not ready. When at last they did come, they found the door was shut. It was too late! A whole new age, typified by a marriage feast, had begun.

Now, they all slept, you remember. Five slept because they hid their heads in the sand and pretended that the world would always be the same, that the human race would continue and things would ever go on as they had. Hiding themselves from the facts of their present situation, they could, of course, dream their way to the moment of the cry, 'Behold, the bridegroom comes!' Whereas the five wise, typifying those who were ready, were not unrealistic escapists who hid their heads from the facts, but those who were prepared to introduce another factor – God, and the fact of God's Word, the fact of God sending Jesus, the fact of Jesus' message which said that, because it was God's world and because it was God who had already come in Christ, he was going to come again and bring it to its conclusion. They went to bed with a peace in their minds

[4] Matthew 25:1–13.

and hearts for they knew their Saviour and knew his Word could be trusted. They knew that the last chapter of *homo sapiens* would not be in the hands of man but in the hands of God who made him, that 'In the beginning God . . .' concludes with 'in the end God'.

Certainly the end of the human race is a possibility, but Christians none the less go to rest with peace. They have heard their Saviour say, 'I will come again and take you to myself' and 'My kingdom will come . . . Pray for it.' Christians have prayed for it through the centuries. 'Your kingdom come. Your will be done on earth as it is in heaven.' Trustfully and peacefully they wait and pray and work for that day, despite the gloom and the threats surrounding us.

Probably

Secondly, a new heaven and a new earth is not only a possibility, but a *probability*, because Jesus' words and the words of the Bible, again and again, have authenticated themselves. The Bible is full of prophecies that have been fulfilled in time. If we go right back to the beginning of the Bible, to the book of Genesis from which I have quoted 'In the beginning God . . .', we also read that mankind would find a Saviour, a Saviour who would be born of the seed of woman,[5] but with no mention of the seed of man. Indeed the father of Jesus is never mentioned in the Bible, for something unusual would be involved in his birth, as God slipped into the stream of humanity and went through the foetal experience to be born as a child. The seed of woman was to come who would bruise the head of man's arch-enemy, the evil power of darkness, and bring to an end Satan's realm of injustice, oppression, hatred, lust, greed, selfishness, pride. Christ's kingdom would come and these things would be bruised and destroyed.

David went through many difficult experiences and recorded them in his psalms, but no experience of David followed the pattern that he outlined in Psalm 22, 'My God, my God, why hast thou forsaken me?. . . They have

[5] Genesis 3:15.

pierced my hands and my feet, they divide my garments among them, and for my raiment they cast lots.' One thousand years before Jesus came, the specific details of the event of the crucifixion are recorded by this prophet, as he spoke of things beyond his experience.

Isaiah tells us that one would be born called 'Emmanuel' – God with us.[6] Such an event would arise in the history of the Jews when God in the flesh would appear. Isaiah proceeds to tell us that this one would be bruised for our sins; he would be wounded for our iniquities; the chastisement of our peace would be upon him, and through his wounds we would be healed. They would 'make his grave with the wicked' but 'in his death with the rich',[7] foretelling how Jesus would be executed with criminals, but they would bury him in the tomb of Joseph of Arimathea, the rich man.

Micah tells us that it would be in Bethlehem that he would be born: 'Bethlehem Ephrathah, who are little to be among the clans of Judah, from you shall come forth for me one who is to be ruler in Israel, whose origin is from of old, from ancient days.'[8] God's promises are fulfilled. There is a high probability that what he has said concerning his second coming will equally, and as specifically, and as precisely, come to pass. Not one iota, says the Lord Jesus, shall pass from what I say, till it is all accomplished. 'Heaven and earth will pass away, but my words will not pass away.'[9]

Plausibly

This brings us to the *plausibility* of Jesus' coming again. The Old Testament says, 'Don't listen to a prophet who prophesies and nothing comes to pass.' In fact it says, 'Execute him, for he is a false prophet.'[10] If any man says, I speak in the name of the Lord, but what he says is not true, because it does not come to pass, then remove him out of your society; don't listen. So the prophets used to prophesy about their immediate concerns, about the injustices of their day and how God would judge them; how

[6] Isaiah 7:14. [7] Isaiah 53:9 [8] Micah 5:2 [9] Mark 13:31. [10] Deuteronomy 18:18–22.

a foreign king would sweep through Israel, how the throne would be overthrown, how God's will would be accomplished. Then and then only would they go on to speak of a distant future and the end of all mankind. So if what they had to say about the immediate future was fulfilled, you took a lot of notice as to what they said about the distant future, when the heaven and earth would pass away.

Similarly, Jesus, when his disciples said, 'Look at this wonderful temple, it has taken forty-six years in building, and look at its precious stones' – for it was the very magnificence of Jerusalem, taking up one sixth of the whole city, built out of the affluence of King Herod; no-one would ever have thought such a building would be brought down, not even by the worst destroyer; it was too beautiful, too aesthetic, let alone the fact (they said) that God had himself founded it – Jesus said, despite the improbability of the situation, 'Not one stone will remain upon another before this generation passes', and so he prophesied of the immediate future. By AD 70 the stones of the temple were brought down by the invading Roman army into the dust. Blood flowed through the streets of Jerusalem, and the destruction Jesus had predicted was fulfilled forty years after his crucifixion.

In view of this we ought to listen to his other words of prophecy concerning the end time, when he goes on to say that just as it was in the days of Noah, men would be eating and drinking, giving in marriage and getting married, building up their businesses, buying and selling . . . then there would come on to the scene of mankind a judgment that would conclude this age. Jesus accurately prophesied the immediate destruction; he has also prophesied the final judgment and end of all things.

In the Old Testament it was reckoned that at the end of this age of mankind the Jews would be brought back into Palestine. Long before ever it came to pass, those who read the Bible said it would, and so it has today. Again, Jesus foretold that his good news would be preached in every nation throughout the world, and only then would the end come; and so it is being done and soon will be concluded. Also it was said in the last book of the Bible that this world order would wind up into one great economic commercial system, figuratively called the 'city of Babylon', whereby all economics flowed into one central head, and the greatest wishes of mankind to have a utopia built on economics would be born. Such is now accepted and worked for by international economists, and many men look to it as the only solution to our world problems.

The unvarnished truth

God in Christ has wrapped himself into our world, into the Jewish world initially, accepting the hatred that goes with that; into the world of illegitimacy, accepting the opprobrium going with that; into the unjust world where he was judged by a false judge; into the world of false witnesses where he was misrepresented and lied about; into the world of toil and pain and sorrow and suffering and death, accepting his own tragic, torturous death. God has been in this world scene, wrapped humanity to himself, his own creation, the very dust of the earth, and through the cross and by the resurrection declares that in the dead end of mankind *there yet will be hope*. For God has already spoken and God has already done something; he can and he will salvage the human race.

The coming again of Jesus Christ is to establish *truth*. The *lie*, says the apostle Paul, which began at the beginning of mankind, led men to serve and worship the creature rather than the Creator, to serve and worship *man* rather than to serve and worship God. That is the *lie* according to the apostle Paul (in Romans chapter 1) – the lie that says, In the beginning *man* . . . and in the end *man* . . . and it worships *man*. The *truth* of course is the reverse: to acknowledge that we are creatures, that God is our Creator, that in the beginning *God* . . . and in the end *God* . . . and in the present moment, now . . . God . . . And I am here for him. In the last of his epistles to the churches, the apostle Paul says, basing his words on what Jesus taught, that at the end of this age there will be a mankind that sets itself up in the place of God, claims a worship above anything that is worshipped, professes itself to be god – and that is called the *lie*, as man worships himself on a full scale. The *truth*, on the other hand, is that God has become man, and Jesus said, '*I am* the *truth*'. The truth is that *God has become man*. The lie is that *man thinks he has become God*. When the truth and the lie finally encounter one another, when Christ interrupts the flow of time and space at his coming again, the anti-god will perish at the brightness of Christ's appearing; for as truth shines into untruth, it destroys it; as love meets unlove, there is a conflagration in which the resistance is consumed, just as when we put on the light the darkness is overcome. The coming kingdom of God is the kingdom of *truth*. The truth is that God has become man, that men might come to God, and not that man might become God!

The new age of Christ is ushered in with a final evaluation of our lives – their goodness, or lack of it. We receive a verdict based on whether our lives have flowed in the stream of truth, or in the stream of the lie. Did we play at being gods and set ourselves up in our own egocentricity, surrounded by our own kingdom, or have we acknowledged the God and Creator of all as central, ever finding him in the Person of his Son, the Lord Jesus Christ, the *truth?* It will be a judgment on the beauty which exists in our inner lives, when they are stripped of our unfortunately inherited dispositions. We will stand before God as naked spirits who have chosen either love or hate, pride or humility, bitterness or forgiveness, oppression or mercy. The inner choice of our spirits will be exposed before the Almighty God. For if love 'builds up'[11] it follows that hatred is destructive and therefore cannot enter the kingdom.

If truth 'sets man free'[12] then untruth would bring man into bondage and must be destroyed. We will stand before God, the small and the great, and the books of our lives will be opened, and our naked spirits will be revealed and

[11] 1 Corinthians 8:1. [12] John 8:32.

exposed to the searchlight of God's eyes: what we *are* will be there, and what we are is what we have done – we cannot change that; and what we have chosen to do is judged as what we wanted to be. Each man will be judged as to whether he is in the new age of the kingdom of our God and of his Christ. God judges in love, for as the heavenly lover, he would bare the soul of the loved one and invade the personality of the one to whom he gives himself.

It is because God is love that he has to search our being, for lovers have no secrets. If we try to keep the pages of our lives closed and protest, 'God, don't read that! Don't look at that! God, I am not this, I am something else', trying to stick the pages of our life down, how can his love get through to us? It is the very love of God that searches and tries.

If I slam shut the book of my life and say, 'For God's sake, leave me alone,' God in his mercy will do so. The only way he can give himself to us is by our receiving him, by giving ourselves to him.

New world

In one of his children's books C. S. Lewis tells the story of two children who were snatched off into another place – I suppose you could compare it to heaven, or God's kingdom. With them is taken a witch, a cabby driver and Uncle Andrew. By chance, the witch has transported a bit of a lamp-post with her on the way. All at once the lion, who represents the Lord Jesus, comes towards them, singing. As he sings, the children and the cabby driver are delighted. 'Gawd,' says the cabby, 'ain't it lovely? Glory be, I'd ha' been a better man all my life if I'd known there were things like this! 'Old your noise, everyone, I want to listen to the moosic.' In contrast, the witch thinks it is the most horrible thing she has ever heard, and throws the metal in her hand at the lion, but it has no effect on him. She screams and flees. Uncle Andrew also wants to get away, but falls over into a stream. The final judgment will be a little like that. The very same 'tune' which will be horrific to some will be heaven to others.

Christ will fill his coming kingdom with the beauty and goodness of truth. This is the 'music' of heaven. To enter this age I need to admit the primacy of these values in my life-style and personal relationships, and acknowledge his verdict on my life where there has been failure in these respects; for I have not lived consistently according to them. Yet this very confession of sin and failure enables the judge of my life to account me fit, nevertheless, to enter the kingdom. One of the pictures of the new age and its entry qualification is found in the last book of the New Testament, the book of Revelation. Here, the New Age is seen as the new Jerusalem, full of God's truth, beauty and goodness; but before we enter the city, a judgment seat has to be passed, by all. Here the books of our lives are opened and we are judged accordingly. Each man is judged according to his works and the just verdict is 'sinner', and the just sentence is 'death'. Yet there is another book, the Lamb's book of *life*, and those who are found in this record are declared right with God and fit to 'enter into the joy of the Lord'.

How can those who have received the sentence of death be found in the book of life? The fact is that if we accept God's judgment on us now and simply plead 'guilty' (not blaming society, heredity, family or environment), we find that God meets us at the place where the sentence was carried out, that is, at Calvary, where Jesus Christ, the Lamb of God, died for us. When we accept that death on our behalf, God enters our name in the Lamb's book of life. Jesus said, 'He who hears my word and believes him who sent me, has eternal life; he shall not come into condemnation but has passed from death to life.' We can be part of God's New Age, by accepting and receiving his truth now. 'You shall know the truth,' says Jesus, 'and the truth shall make you *free*.' Free to step out into the future with him who was there at the foundation of our world, and will be there at its end to lead us into the new Jerusalem, the New Age.